The HANDBOOK *for a* HAPPY CAT

Speak Their Language, Decode Their Quirks, and Meet Their Needs—*So They'll Love You Back!*

LIESBETH PUTS

Translated by Maria Danielson

THE EXPERIMENT

NEW YORK

THE HANDBOOK FOR A HAPPY CAT: *Speak Their Language, Decode Their Quirks, and Meet Their Needs—So They'll Love You Back!*
Copyright © 2019 by Liesbeth Puts/Kosmos Publishers, Utrecht/Antwerp
Translation copyright © 2021 by The Experiment, LLC

First published by Kosmos Publishers, The Netherlands, in 2019 as *Als de kat het voor het zeggen had.* This edition published by arrangement with Shared Stories. First published in English in North America in revised form by The Experiment, LLC, in 2021.

The Experiment, LLC | 220 East 23rd Street, Suite 600 | New York, NY 10010-4658
theexperimentpublishing.com

This book is sold with the understanding that neither the author nor the publisher is engaged in rendering personal professional services. It is not a substitute for consultation with a veterinarian or feline behavioral therapist. The author and publisher specifically disclaim all responsibility for any liability, loss, or risk—personal or otherwise—incurred as a direct or indirect consequence of the use of this book or its contents, which are the author's ideas and opinions. Always contact your veterinarian or a behavioral therapist with concerns about your cat's health or well-being.

THE EXPERIMENT and its colophon are registered trademarks of The Experiment, LLC. Many of the designations used by manufacturers and sellers to distinguish their products are claimed as trademarks. Where those designations appear in this book and The Experiment was aware of a trademark claim, the designations have been capitalized.

The Experiment's books are available at special discounts when purchased in bulk for premiums and sales promotions as well as for fund-raising or educational use. For details, contact us at info@theexperimentpublishing.com.

Library of Congress Cataloging-in-Publication Data

Names: Puts, Liesbeth, author.
Title: The handbook for a happy cat : speak their language, decode their quirks, and meet their needs--so they'll love you back! / Liesbeth Puts ; translated by Maria Danielson.
Other titles: Als de kat het voor het zeggen had. English
Description: New York : The Experiment, 2021. | Includes index. | Summary: "An easy-reference guide to cat care and psychology filled with irresistible photos"-- Provided by publisher.
Identifiers: LCCN 2021027350 (print) | LCCN 2021027351 (ebook) | ISBN 9781615197101 (paperback) | ISBN 9781615197118 (ebook)
Subjects: LCSH: Cats--Psychology. | Cats--Behavior. | Cats.
Classification: LCC SF446.5 .P8813 2021 (print) | LCC SF446.5 (ebook) | DDC 636.8/083--dc23
LC record available at https://lccn.loc.gov/2021027350
LC ebook record available at https://lccn.loc.gov/2021027351

ISBN 978-1-61519-710-1
Ebook ISBN 978-1-61519-711-8

Cover and additional text design by Beth Bugler
Text design by Femke den Hertog
Photographs on pages 5 (top), 8 (right), 14, 15, 21, 22 (top), 23, 24 (top), 25 (top), 29, 36, 52, 76, 77, 91, 110, 112, 119, 137, and 197 copyright © Warren Photographic
Photographs on pages 9 and 46 copyright © Madeleine Gimpel and Femke den Hertog
Photographs on pages 113 and 131 copyright © Sure Petcare
Photograph on page 158 copyright © Erwin Puts
Photographs on cover, pages 41, 44, and 92 by iStock
All other photographs by Shutterstock

Manufactured in Turkey

First printing October 2021
10 9 8 7 6 5 4 3 2 1

*In loving memory of my brother Erwin
and my very special cat Dennis*

CONTENTS

PREFACE

The famous Dutch biologist Midas Dekkers was once asked what he would say to his cat if he could ask her just one question. Dekkers replied, "Are you happy?" He is not the only one to ponder this question. Every cat owner would like to have a happy cat in their home.

How can you tell if a cat is happy? This, it turns out, is not a simple matter. We think of cats as beautiful, unique, elegant, and cuddly, but they are also mysterious, unpredictable, and even absolutely incomprehensible. Cats are not very communicative. It is not for nothing that there are countless books about the enigma of cats, and the internet is full of stories about cats and their behavior.

The answer is simple: You make a cat happy by getting to know him. Once you understand him better, you will know what your cat really needs in his day-to-day life. You might think that he will automatically be happy if you transform your house into a kitty playground, keep the house at the ideal temperature, and buy the perfect collection of toys. However, it is much more important to look at your cat's needs from the perspective of his natural behavior. Lest we forget: Cats will be cats!

That is precisely what this book is about: How can you ensure that your cat can be herself? For this book I took a deep dive into the literature, critically reading countless books and recent scientific articles. I have translated this information into practical, actionable tips and insights about your cat. Your cat's body language and senses, how to interact with your cat (or "catiquette"), relationships between cats, and the importance of play are just a few of the topics covered. This book will answer many of your questions about your cat.

I hope this book inspires you to look at your cat in a new light and to understand him (even better). After all, you would do anything for your cat's well-being and happiness, wouldn't you?

PART 1

What is a cat?

HOW DOES A CAT PERCEIVE THE WORLD?

A cat is a hunter, there is no doubt about that. The fact that she is a hunter determines her behavior, her appearance, and how she perceives the world. How she sees the world, in turn, determines how she reacts to you. Many misunderstandings between humans and cats arise because we do not actually have the foggiest idea how a cat perceives her surroundings. For us, sight is very important, and we communicate with others primarily by talking. For a cat, scent is paramount, and he communicates primarily with body language.

You can understand your cat's behavior much better if you know how his senses work.

SMELL

Smell is the most important sense for a cat, and a cat's sense of smell is much better than ours. Scientists don't know exactly how many different scents a cat can distinguish, but there must be thousands.

A cat can "smell" in two different ways.

NOSE

The nose is used to detect scents in the environment: food, prey, other animals, and the like. A cat is so good at distinguishing between different smells that a recent article suggested cats could possibly be trained for search-and-rescue operations. Their smaller size and flexibility would allow cats access to places where a search-and-rescue dog can't go (Shreve & Udell, 2017).

Cats can probably also recognize chemical changes in their owners' bodies. Just think of cats who respond differently to a woman when she is pregnant!

MOUTH

Apart from her nose, a cat has an additional scent organ to perceive pheromones (as opposed to other scents), called the *vomeronasal organ* or *Jacobson's organ*. It is a split in the roof of the mouth, directly behind the front teeth. Perhaps you've seen your cat sniff an object and then open her mouth, making a face as if disgusted. This is called the *flehmen response* and it actually opens the vomeronasal organ. A cat will do this only when she is triggered by a particular smell, usually urine.

Why cats have these two different olfactory systems is not yet one hundred percent clear, but we know that a cat's vomeronasal organ is devoted exclusively to analyzing the smells of other cats.

The flehmen response

PHEROMONES

Animals use pheromones to communicate with each other or to evoke a specific reaction. Pheromones are "species-specific," that is, cats can only detect the pheromones of other cats. A cat emits pheromones from scent glands located on her head (under the chin, near the cheeks, at the corners of the mouth, and near the ears), between her toes, around her anus, and where her back meets her tail. Urine also contains pheromones.

SNIFFING

Cats often preface their interactions by sniffing each other, even if they have known one another a long time. That's why it's so important to help cats exchange smells as a first step when introducing a new cat to a group (see page 69). Cats recognize each other by their scents.

COMMUNICATION

Cats communicate through smell—for example, by rubbing their cheeks or head along an object, scratching things, leaving their poop in a

conspicuous place, and of course by spraying (see page 59).

The advantage of leaving your scent somewhere is that the "message" remains recognizable for a few days, even when you are not around. This makes sense considering cats' evolution as solitary animals: Leaving your scent is a more effective way of communicating than, say, meowing: It's like posting an ad on the grocery-store bulletin board. A cat

Top: A quick check to see who this other cat is

Left: This cat is investigating the smells another cat has left behind

in heat, for example, can make it clear that she's on the prowl for a fine feline. A tomcat can smell that his arch enemy two yards over is ill (and thus perhaps vulnerable).

Although cats live much more closely together today (by necessity) than they did thousands of years ago, scent is still their most important way to tell each other something. Evolutionary changes don't happen very fast.

HEARING

A cat's ears are extraordinary. The triangular outer ear, or *pinna*, and the ridged inner ear function together as a type of complex amplifier. A cat can move her two ears independently and turn them nearly 180 degrees, enabling her to better locate her prey.

Unsurprisingly, cats have a much keener sense of hearing than we do. A cat's range—10.5 octaves versus a human's 9.3 octaves—is the largest of

The ridges inside a cat's ear contribute to her keen hearing

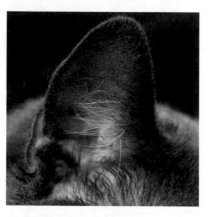

any mammal's. That might not seem like much more, but the difference lies in the sounds at the top and the bottom of the spectrum, which we can't hear. The high frequencies, in the ultrasonic range, are particularly interesting: A cat can hear bats clicking and the high-pitched squeaking of mice, their natural prey.

Thanks to her "amplifiers," a cat can also hear the soft rustling noises of a mouse hidden in the grass. The drawback is that cats experience loud noises much more intensely than we do. It's no wonder that so many cats are terribly frightened by fireworks.

VISION

A cat's eyes are relatively large in proportion to its head. This has one big disadvantage, namely, that they are harder to focus. Objects within about 1 foot of her nose are fuzzy to a cat; objects farther away than 18 feet or so are also blurry. A cat doesn't need to see prey that far away. And because a cat does not see well close up, she uses her whiskers when catching prey (see page 8).

A cat's eyes also adapt to her environment. Cats who grow up indoors are often near-sighted, whereas outdoor cats are usually a bit far-sighted (Bradshaw, 2012).

An outdoor cat catches many small prey animals (mice, birds) every day, so she sets out multiple times a day to hunt. She does this in broad daylight as well as at dusk and dawn, which requires some special adaptations.

At dusk, a cat's pupils widen so they can absorb extra light. In addition, cats have a special layer behind the retina, the *tapetum lucidum*, that reflects light. You will see this light up, for example, when a cat looks into a car's headlights at night. This adaptation helps the cat make the most of a small amount of light. A cat can't see a thing when it is completely dark; there always has to be a source of light. In other words, cats are not truly nocturnal; they are regularly busy hunting or playing during the day.

Cats' eyes have a relatively high number of light-sensitive cells (rods) but only two types of color-sensitive cells (cones). The rods ensure that the cat can spot rapid movements especially well and can see in the dark. On the other hand, they can absorb too much light during the day. To protect his eyes during the day, his pupils constrict to narrow slits.

Being able to see movement is much more important to a cat than seeing colors. He only distinguishes between the colors blue and green. So you don't need to worry at all about whether your cat likes the color of his litterbox or toys.

Biologists discovered fairly recently that cats can see ultraviolet light. Until then, people thought that only insects (such as bees), fish, amphibians, reptiles, and a few particular mammals (mice, rats, and bats among them) could do so. It is not yet clear what advantage this offers to a cat.

Top: The *tapetum lucidum* lights up when you use a flash

Left: Narrowed pupils protect a cat's eyes from too much sunlight

The short hairs between the toes make a cat's feet very sensitive

TOUCH

Cats have a highly developed sense of touch.

The soles of a cat's feet are much more sensitive than you might think. This is because of the tiny hairs between her toes. A cat's foot pads convey a lot of information to her: What sort of surface is she walking on, and is it firm enough for her to jump toward her prey? The cat may also feel the

Why doesn't a cat see toys right in front of her face?

A cat cannot see clearly from a short distance, and she barely sees any colors (she is better at observing movement). So, she will hardly notice a toy that does not move, especially against a background of a similar color.

vibrations of prey scurrying across the ground. This sensitivity explains why a cat does not like to have her feet touched.

The whiskers are tactile organs, too, and communicate a lot of sensory information to a cat. Each whisker is embedded in a follicle that contains muscles, nerve receptors, and so on. The cat feels even the slightest touch.

Because a cat's whiskers are so sensitive, it is best to consider this when choosing a food and water bowl (see page 120). Some cats don't like eating from a small bowl because their whiskers will brush against the sides. There is even a term for this: *whisker stress.*

Right: You can easily see the vibrissae above this cat's eyes

Below: When prey is within reach, a cat points her whiskers forward

Whiskers are elemental to hunting. They come into play when a cat's prey comes too close for her to see it clearly. At that moment, she sweeps her whiskers forward. When they touch her prey, her claws take over and grab it with deadly precision. Whiskers are very important to a cat: You must never clip them, even if they are very long.

Besides whiskers, a cat has other long hairs on her head called *vibrissae.* You can find them above the eyes and above the whiskers on either side. A cat also has a small group of hairs at the back of each front paw.

These probably play a role in hunting: They are just as sensitive as the whiskers and help the cat detect his prey—especially when hunting at dusk. (Big cats that hunt only during the day, such as cheetahs, do not have these *carpal vibrissae*.)

TASTE

Cats have the reputation of being picky, and it's true that they have specific dietary requirements. By nature, cats always catch live prey; they are not scavengers. Their sense of taste is not very acute, but the smell of food, of course, plays a big role. Cats seems to prefer smells that resemble meat—that is, foods with a lot of fat and protein.

Like us, cats have taste buds on their tongue to detect certain basic flavors—sour, bitter, and salty. Unlike us, a cat cannot taste sweetness. Although some cats like to partake of pudding or whipped cream, being able to taste sweetness is of little value to a carnivore.

Cats do taste bitterness, however. For example, they have many receptors that respond to quinine (the bitter taste in tonic). In nature, bitterness almost always indicates a toxic substance, so many animals avoid it.

Does a cat use her whiskers to see if she fits somewhere?

This is an oft-repeated theory, but is it true? After all, cats regularly get stuck in spaces that are too small. Also, the length of their whiskers is determined genetically. Some breeds don't have whiskers, or have extremely short ones. It is more likely that whiskers play a role in navigation at dusk and in the dark.

WHAT YOUR CAT IS TELLING YOU: BODY LANGUAGE

A cat is a hunter, there is no doubt about that. A cat communicates with other cats primarily through scent, but also through body language. An animal that lives a solitary life (as cats originally did) is vulnerable: If it gets injured in a fight and cannot hunt anymore, it's finished. So, a cat will do everything in his power to avoid a fight with another cat, and a lot of his body language is aimed at keeping his distance from other cats. A good observer can recognize a cat's intention from afar. If an enemy still comes too close, the cat can reinforce his body language by growling or snarling.

Learning your cat's body language is an important way to recognize how your cat is feeling. But cats don't always make it easy for us to understand them, because the context in which they find themselves also plays a role!

EYES
PUPIL SIZE
The size of a cat's pupils provides a great example of the importance of context: A frightened cat has large pupils, but so does a cat in a dimly lit room. The latter case has nothing to do with fear; the pupils enlarge to absorb as much light as possible.

When a cat has large pupils in a tense situation, he is clearly afraid or agitated.

When cats are hunting or fighting, their pupils will suddenly widen just before they attack.

STARING

Staring is a form of aggression in cat language. Cats who do not like one another can stare at each other for a long time. Usually, this signals that a fight is about to break out. One of the cats might start walking away in slow motion to avoid a confrontation. (I discuss averting catfights on page 71.)

Cats can stare at people, too, which is also often a prelude to aggression. Some people think it is a fun game to see who can last the longest without looking away, but a cat does not really think this is fun.

Can you look at a cat?

You may read somewhere on the internet that you shouldn't look at a cat. That is nonsense, of course. A cat watches her surroundings closely by nature, and she looks at you to observe your behavior. A well-socialized cat will make eye contact with you, particularly if she wants something, such as food or attention. She knows exactly what she must do to make that happen.

In our western culture, it is customary for people to look each other in the eyes when talking, but long "conversations" can be a bit too pushy for a cat. The precise line between looking and staring will differ from cat to cat.

BLINKING

You can de-escalate tense situations with scared or aggressive cats by clearly looking away or turning your head. Another option is to slowly close your eyes and open them again, the "slow blink." For a cat, this is a clear signal that you mean him no harm. If you do this a few times in a row, you may see that the cat blinks back at you as an answer, or even relaxes. For people who work with frightened cats at a shelter, this is always a beautiful moment, a real breakthrough.

Sometimes you can calm an aggressive cat down by slow-blinking at him, especially if you do this at the first sign of aggression.

A frightened cat: big pupils, flattened ears, crouching with the tail wrapped around the body

Cats also blink at each other. They are signaling they will leave one another alone—for example, if cats in a group want to rest after eating. Cats can also blink as a calming signal in situations where tension has suddenly escalated.

EARS

Cats' ears move a lot. The ears can move independently of each other so the cat can better pinpoint the location of her prey. Even when a cat is relaxing, her ears will still turn to catch sounds.

FORWARD

When the ears are facing forward, the cat is alert.

BACKWARD

When a cat turns his ears backward it often signals aggression, but it could also be that he does not trust the situation.

AGAINST THE HEAD

Partially flattened ears are a sign of fear, and ears flattened so closely against the head that you barely see them are an expression of extreme fear. Cats fold their ears backward or against the head to protect the fragile inner ear from injury during a fight.

WHISKERS

Like the ears, a cat's whiskers move swiftly and in many directions. They are not the best indicator of your cat's emotions. It's best to consider them as just one element of your cat's overall posture.

NEUTRAL POSITION

When a cat is relaxed, his whiskers will be in a neutral position, at a 90-degree angle to his nose.

HANGING DOWN

When cats are very relaxed, their whiskers point or hang downward. Personally, I call this the "walrus position."

FORWARD

A cat who is playing or chasing prey points his whiskers forward to help him hunt. A curious, alert cat or a cat who is coming to say hello will also point his whiskers forward. To make things even more confusing, an aggressive cat will also point his whiskers forward!

FLAT AGAINST THE CHEEKS

A frightened cat will press his whiskers flat against his cheeks to protect them from injury during a fight.

THE TAIL

UP

A tail sticking up in the air signals that a cat has seen you. Sometimes she will come greet you (or another cat), in which case her tail has a slight curve at the end, like a question mark. Or she might just raise her tail while walking by, without making any further contact.

When a cat sprays, he backs up to an object and stands with his tail quivering, and sometimes he treads with his hind legs. Urine is sprayed out horizontally. You might see a cat "going through the motions," but without urine coming out, which is usually a sign of positive excitement. Your cat might do this while waiting for his food.

This cat is coming to greet you with his tail in the air

The cat on the left is showing aggression; the one on the right is frightened

15

DOWN

When a cat is relaxed, his tail hangs down. A cat with his tail between his legs is afraid. However, this behavior does not indicate submission or surrender.

BUSHY TAIL

A bushy tail ("bottle brush") is often a sign of fear or uncertainty. The tail of an aggressive cat looks different (see photo, page 15). It can be puffed up, but often you will see that only the hairs at the base are standing. The tail of an aggressive cat makes a (more or less) 90-degree angle with the spine.

SWISHING TAIL

A cat will swish her tail in various ways and for various reasons.

She may move her tail back and forth very slowly. This means your cat is content. You will see this with cats who are eating, or relaxing on the couch. Depending on the situation, this can also indicate that something has caught her attention.

If your cat is on your lap and starts flicking her tail more vigorously, it is very likely that she has had enough petting and is getting irritated. You'll often see this in combination with ears that turn backward.

Cats who want to impress each other move the entire tail slowly from left to right and back again to appear larger.

A cat who "chatters" at a bird and swishes his tail wildly in all directions is expressing excitement.

A cat who sees a bird can swish its tail wildly

Some cats "thump" their tails, slapping the ground loud enough for you to hear. This is usually a sign of extreme discontent and sometimes even aggression.

That said, you might also see a cat "thump" whose body language is otherwise relaxed. The reason for this is not really known; it might have to do with past (traumatic) experiences that have left the cat still feeling somewhat anxious.

WALKING

How a cat walks through a room says something about how she feels. A self-confident cat takes the shortest route from A to B, whereas a frightened or uncertain cat prefers to walk along the walls, avoiding the open middle area of a room.

RELAXED

A cat who feels comfortable in his skin will have a stretched-out back, alert ears, and a relaxed tail hanging down, or sometimes half raised.

ANXIOUS

An anxious or scared cat will walk with his back lowered and his belly to the ground, while staying very alert and constantly turning his ears to quickly locate danger. (Pain can also contribute to an abnormal way of walking.)

ASSERTIVE/AGGRESSIVE

An assertive or aggressive cat walks with stiff front paws, her back arching upward, and her head lowered, laser-focused on the other person or animal.

SOUNDS

A cat has a whole range of sounds. As with body language, the noises a cat makes can mean different things at different times.

HISSING

Cats who are startled, especially those who are anxious in general, can hiss both at people and at other cats. Hissing is mainly intended to keep the other person or cat at a distance—to say "leave me alone!" In that case it is best to leave her be. A cat may hiss if you touch him somewhere that hurts. He might also growl, especially if the fear or pain is intense.

There are also cats who hiss before vomiting.

YOWLING

Yowling is another possible sign of aggression, often used when cats want to demonstrate their strength to potential enemies. By nature, cats would rather not fight; this way, they hope to avoid a confrontation.

GROWLING

Some cats growl while eating, particularly if they have been served something especially delicious. Cats are not accustomed to sharing, so if they have "caught"

Hissing can be a sign of fear

something tasty or special, they would rather keep other cats at a distance. In this case, growling is a warning.

There are cats who growl when they are holding a particular toy.

CHATTERING

A cat who sees a bird makes a characteristic "chattering" sound. This sound varies a lot from cat to cat: Some cats sing entire arias; others chatter their teeth; and others silently open and close their mouths. No thorough research has been conducted into why cats do this, but there are strong indications that it's a sign of excitement upon spotting prey. Domestic cats aren't the only ones to chatter; lions and lynxes do it, too.

It is thought that the Margay cat from Brazil mimics monkeys to attract them and catch them.

MEOWING

You won't hear a feral cat meowing. For a solitary animal, just calling out into the forest doesn't serve any purpose. Domestic cats can talk a lot, though—especially to their owners.

Kittens meow at their mother when they have strayed too far from the litter. Some researchers say that our pet cats are really still kittens at heart and consider us their mother, but that is difficult to prove.

Another, much more logical explanation is surprisingly simple: A cat meows because we talk back. Meowing is thus learned behavior: A cat quickly finds that meowing is the very best way to get an owner's attention. Siamese cats and other Eastern breeds are known to be quite chatty, and usually loud to boot.

When a cat meows, we tend to talk back

A cat has an entire repertoire of meows, specific to the individual. As an owner, you may think you have a good understanding of your cat's meows—but in fact, you likely understand each meow because of context: A piercing meow at the closed kitchen door is a clear hint. It gets a bit more difficult when you can't see your cat: Research has shown that when owners don't see their pets and only hear them on tape, their ability to interpret their own cat's meow is much lower (Ellis, 2015).

Does a cat meow when in pain?

A cat in pain will withdraw and may meow—but not necessarily. A cat who isn't meowing can still be in pain (see page 201).

PURRING

Nearly all cats purr, although they may do it so quietly that you can't hear it. All of the smaller wildcat species can also purr; whereas big cats like lions, tigers, and leopards don't.

About twenty years ago, scientists figured out exactly what is going on physiologically while a cat is purring. By building up and then releasing tension, the vocal larynx of the cat closes and reopens. This suddenly separates the vocal cords, causing the purring sound. A cat purrs both upon inhale and exhale. Between breaths, the cat takes a break for a fraction of a second, but to us it sounds like one continuous purr.

Kittens

Kittens start purring when they are a few days old; they do it while nursing from their mother. It may simply be an expression of contentment. The alternative theory is that purring, which is almost always coupled with the front paws rhythmically "kneading," is a way to stimulate milk flow.

Since kittens are born deaf and blind, they cannot hear their mother, but they can feel the vibrations when she purrs and find her that way. Of course, a mama cat could also be purring simply because she is content.

Adult cats purr mainly when they are interacting with other cats or people.

Pain?

Although we usually think of purring as an expression of contentment, cats can also purr when in intense pain—for example, after a serious injury or during labor. Some people interpret the purring of an injured cat at the vet as a sign that she wants to keep living, but it's more likely that she is just trying to comfort herself. Cats can even purr at the very end of the process of dying.

THE "SOLICITING PURR"

Researchers have confirmed that not all purrs sound the same (McComb, 2009). Sometimes the purring noise has a high-pitched, voiced component, reminiscent of a cry or meow. This "soliciting purr" is used, for example, when a cat wants to be fed: It is more urgent than normal purring. It has not been observed in kittens or feral cats, so it is very likely a learned behavior.

How loudly can a cat purr?

There are cats who purr nearly silently; you have to lay a finger on their throat to feel the vibrations. On the other end of the spectrum, there are highly audible cats. The tomcat Merlin (from Devon, Great Britain) holds the record for the world's loudest purr. He purrs at a whopping 67.8 decibels—that's as loud as a dishwasher or a clothes dryer!

This kitten's arched back tells us she is very afraid

Afraid or aggressive?

AFRAID

- Big pupils (black eyes).
- Ears flattened.
- Whiskers flat against the cheeks.
- A crouched posture with the tail folded around the body; in extreme fear the cat might "freeze."
- The cat recoils; this cat will attack if she cannot flee.
- Sometimes, an arched back with a fluffed tail (the classic "Halloween cat"). This is an attempt to make herself look bigger in the hopes of scaring off her opponent.
- Belly low to the ground.
- A very frightened cat may pant or even hyperventilate.
- Hissing is almost always a sign of fear. When a cat is really scared, she may also growl.

AGGRESSIVE

- The pupils are narrowed to slits (to protect them from injury during a fight).
- The ears are turned backward (not flattened).
- The whiskers are pointed forward or turned downward.
- The hairs on the back part of the back are slightly raised.
- The tail bends down from the spine at a 90-degree angle and might be partially fluffed.
- The cat walks with stiff front paws.
- The tail swishes back and forth.
- An aggressive cat might hiss, but usually will growl and sometimes yowl.

ANXIOUS OR AGGRESSIVE?

If you aren't sure whether a cat is scared or aggressive, remember this: An aggressive cat wants to make an impression, stays focused on the adversary, and will walk toward them; whereas a frightened cat will crouch or hunker down. That may seem clear on paper, but in real life you'll probably see a combination of fear and aggression. Not every cat exhibits the signs described above in exactly the same way.

Kittens display all kinds of "aggressive" behavior during play. A young kitten will sometimes walk sideways toward another kitten (or her owner), arch her back, or puff up her tail. This is most likely practice for later, and some cats never outgrow this behavior.

ROLLING OR LYING ON THEIR BACK

A cat who lies or rolls on his back is not submissive! On the contrary, he has all his claws and his strong back paws ready to defend himself and is a dangerous opponent. When young cats lie on their back, it is a challenge to play.

Some cats will lie or roll on their back when they want their stomach petted, but just as often a cat will grab your hand and start kicking your arm with his back legs—making clear that petting was an unwelcome intimacy at that moment. It is best to respect this boundary; that way

Showing the belly is not always an invitation to pet the cat!

you'll also avoid teaching the cat to play with your hands.

There are also cats who lie or sleep on their back with their legs spread. Of course, that has nothing to do with aggression or submission, but is all about relaxation.

Rolling on the ground can be a positive social gesture for a cat, both toward humans and other cats. It's a compliment if your cat rolls around a lot when you come home!

22

KNEADING ("MAKING BISCUITS")

Kittens or cats "knead" things with their front paws when they feel happy. Cats prefer to knead soft surfaces, such as a pillow, a sweater, or your own belly or legs. This behavior stems primarily from when they were nursing: Kittens stimulate milk release with this motion when they suckle at their mother's side.

Some cats retain this behavior for their entire lives. This is unrelated to how old your cat was when taken from his mother as a kitten. It is a sign that he feels happy and safe.

If your cat has sharp claws, his kneading can be painful. In that case, you can keep his claws short or carefully move him to a pillow or another soft surface. Never punish your cat for this behavior, even if he does cause (unintentional) pain.

Kittens knead with their forepaws when they nurse from their mother

SUCKING

There are kittens and cats who regularly suck on their own tail, paws, or nipples, as well as their owner's hair, sweaters, or blankets. We know relatively little about this behavior, and there may be multiple causes.

TAKEN AWAY FROM THE MOTHER TOO EARLY?

Weaning takes place when kittens are between six and eight weeks old. If this process is abruptly ended—for example, because a kitten is taken from her mother at five or six weeks—there is a chance that she will continue to suckle on soft objects. It's not necessarily the case that every kitten from one litter will exhibit this behavior, just as not every child in a family will suck their thumb.

CONTENT OR STRESSED OUT?

Nursing from their mother is a beautifully warm, safe experience for kittens, for which sucking can be a replacement. Some kittens want to nurse now and then even after weaning, sometimes up until six months of age, or older still.

Confusingly, this same behavior can stem from stress and uncertainty. Just as children may suck their thumbs to comfort themselves, cats (probably) do this to calm themselves down.

A kitten sucking
on a blanket

GENETICS

Some breeds are known for wool-sucking—for example, Siamese and other Eastern breeds.

SHOULD YOU DO ANYTHING ABOUT IT?

As long as this habit does not get out of hand (injured skin, infected nipples), it's not a problem. Some owners try to stop this behavior by bottle-feeding their kitten for a while. However, once she is already eating solid food, this will hardly ever work.

Of course, you should never punish your cat for sucking. Combatting this behavior will only lead to frustration, since the urge to nurse won't go away. A better option is to distract her—with a toy, for example.

HEAD-BUTTING AND MARKING

By rubbing against something or pushing his head against something, a cat leaves his scent, which is oh-so-important, and feels safer. These scent traces must be regularly refreshed because otherwise the smell wears off—even without all our "helpful" dusting and cleaning, which removes that valuable scent.

OBJECTS

Often when a cat appears to rub his cheek against objects in the house, he is actually rubbing his lips against them, and he will usually mark the lowest objects by rubbing them with his chin.

When there is tension between cats or fear of cats outside, your cat will increase his scent-marking to give himself a feeling of safety.

HEAD-BUTTING

When your cat comes to you or sits next to you on the couch, she may push her forehead against your cheek or chin. This can vary from a light touch to a firm head-butt and is

A cat scent-marking a chair

To really understand a cat, you always have to look at the whole cat!

always intended to be friendly. She reserves this behavior for cats, humans, and other animals with whom she has a good bond. Leaving her scent behind is a social gesture.

Some cats use this type of head-butt as an attention-seeking behavior because owners generally respond enthusiastically to this expression of affection.

GREETING

When you come home, your cat will come to greet you. He might stand on his back legs and give you head-butts, or he might push up against your legs, curl his tail around your calves, and rub against you. This does not mean that he wants to make you his "possession," as is often thought; it is rather a form of greeting. Scientists are still in doubt about whether this behavior has to do with sharing scent.

YAWNING

A cat will yawn luxuriantly and stretch out when she wakes up. However, yawning can also have quite a different meaning—namely, stress or tension. For example, you may see your cats yawn when it does not seem fitting. We call this "displacement activity." You might notice this when two cats are staring at each other (negative tension) or when one is waiting to be fed (positive). Yawning releases the tension.

GROOMING

Cats are clean animals who spend about 25 to 30 percent of the day grooming themselves. This serves several functions.

THE CAT'S TONGUE

A cat's tongue is an important tool for grooming. It is covered with small, backward-pointing *papillae*. These help the cat remove loose hair, dust, and other things from his coat that shouldn't be there. A healthy coat should look shiny and sleek, without matting.

The drawback to his tongue's structure is that if he swallows a string or thread, he cannot vomit it up, possibly leading to stomach or intestinal problems.

A cat's rough tongue also serves him well when eating: The papillae clean every last morsel of meat from the bones of his prey.

On hot days, licking their fur helps cats cool off by creating evaporation.

A cat's tongue is covered with papillae

HAIRBALLS

Cats can swallow quite a bit of loose hair while licking and grooming. Most of it is passed in their poop, but if there is way too much, it comes out the other way: as the famous hairball. If that happens once in a while, it's no problem: It's a natural way to get rid of that hair. This might be a reason why cats occasionally eat grass or other plants—to help themselves throw up.

Long-haired cats tend to have more trouble with hairballs than their short-haired counterparts. When the seasons change, your cat may start shedding, losing more hair and thus throwing up more often. But if your cat vomits daily or is clearly feeling sick or uncomfortable for a while after expelling a hairball, it is important to see your veterinarian as soon as possible.

GROOMING EACH OTHER (ALLOGROOMING)

Grooming also has an important social function: When cats feel comfortable and safe in each other's company, they will give each other a bath. This reinforces their social bond, although some cats are clearly more keen on engaging in this behavior than others. Usually allogrooming is limited to the head and shoulders, except between very close friends.

Cats spend a lot of time grooming their fur

Why does my cat lick my hair?

Your cat might think you are due for a cleaning, too, and may lick your hair, hands, or arms. Researchers do not (yet) know what this means, but it might just be similar to allogrooming, a sign that she likes you a lot.

Another explanation is that your cat likes your shampoo, body lotion, or cream, which might contain an ingredient your cat finds attractive. There are also cats who want to lick you mainly when you are sweaty.

Finally, it could be attention-seeking behavior, especially when she does it at a moment your attention is elsewhere.

EXCESSIVE GROOMING

Although grooming is natural behavior and takes up a lot of your cat's time, some cats just go too far. They start licking their fur obsessively, until they have bare patches or (in severe cases) open sores. You might not notice these at first; owners often discover them by accident while brushing or petting their cats.

Although it is often said that excessive grooming is the result of stress, in fact it has an underlying medical cause in the vast majority of cases. This should always be ruled out first.

FLEAS

Fleas are the number-one suspect when we observe bald spots. Even if you don't see any fleas on your cat, he may have been bitten and developed an allergic reaction. A hypersensitive cat may groom himself so well that you never see his fleas (or any flea droppings, which look like little black flecks of "dirt"). So don't rule out that your cat might have fleas without consulting a vet.

ALLERGIES

Allergies or hypersensitivities are another common cause—triggered by certain foods, dust, or pollen (yes, for cats, too)! Unfortunately, blood testing for allergies does not always give a reliable result.

PAIN

If a cat experiences pain somewhere in her body, she might well keep grooming that spot until she loses her hair. The location of the bald spot may tell you something about the underlying cause. For instance, if it is on the stomach, that's often a sign of bladder problems (urinary tract disease or infection). A bald patch on the hips might be caused by osteoarthritis.

STRESS

"Stress" becomes the diagnosis only when your vet hasn't found anything else wrong during a thorough examination. Skin problems or allergies are not easy to diagnose, so don't give up too soon!

BOREDOM

Grooming each other is social behavior

A bored cat may resort to overgrooming, too. Licking creates a happy feeling (specifically, a rush of endorphins), causing her to do it more often. This is comparable to what we call "stereotypic" behavior in zoo animals: repetitive, nonproductive activities like constant pacing. If you think your kitty might be bored, you can easily solve this by engaging in playtime more often (see page 178)!

Licking creates a happy feeling

WHY CATS SLEEP SO MUCH

Cats sleep for much of the day, just like many other predators. Hunting takes a lot of energy, as does patrolling your territory. The more ground you cover, the more you need to eat, and thus hunt, to replenish your energy. Sleeping is the best way to conserve energy in between bursts of activity.

SLEEPING POSITIONS

Cats can sleep in the strangest positions. The most common is curled up, with the tail wrapped around. There are cats who lie their stomach, stretched out on the arm of the couch, and others who lie on their back. Temperature also plays a role: The colder it is, the more likely your cat will curl up like a ball.

Can cats dream?

Deep in sleep, cats twitch their paws, ears, and whiskers. It is as if they are dreaming about chasing prey. Cats do this during REM (rapid eye movement) sleep, and when people are woken up during REM sleep, they often say they were dreaming. Unfortunately, we can't ask a cat . . . but chances are good that he is, in fact, dreaming.

PLEASE DON'T DISTURB

In the wild, cats are always looking for a safe place to sleep. They do *not* want an enemy to attack while they are sleeping. It's the same at home: It will stress a cat out if she is regularly, rudely awoken by children wanting to play or owners wanting to pet her. Teach your children early on that your cat really needs her beauty sleep!

PRETENDING TO SLEEP

Older cats naturally sleep more than younger cats do, but sleeping a lot can also indicate pain, caused by osteoarthritis or other disorders.

Cats who are sick, in pain, or don't feel well may also pretend to sleep: They appear to be sleeping, but their eyes are still slightly open. If you catch your cat doing this, it's worth mentioning to your vet.

Cats love sleeping and do a lot of it!

5

STRESS

Naturally, you want your cat to feel as happy as possible. Stress shouldn't come into it. But cats are so often thought to be easily stressed out—and sometimes they truly are—that I'll devote this entire section to stress.

WHAT IS STRESS?

To put it simply, stress is a survival mechanism. If you come nose to nose with a lion, you have to make a split-second decision to either run away or wage battle. This is the fight-or-flight response. Your body undergoes all kinds of rapid changes, including a surge of adrenaline, to enable you to run or strike back. This is short-term or "acute" stress. Visiting the vet, boarding, moving, and renovating the house are common examples of things that can cause (hopefully) short-term stress for cats.

You can hardly prevent this sort of stress, and that is not necessarily bad. A bit of stress keeps one alert. It may even boost performance, such as when you have a looming deadline. Of course, cats never have

This cat is clearly stressed out and withdrawn

deadlines—but a lack of stress can actually lead to boredom in animals.

Stress is only problematic if the body does not return to a state of rest after the spike in adrenaline. As in people, chronic stress in cats can lead to all kinds of disorders, including diabetes and skin conditions.

HOW DOES A CAT BECOME STRESSED OUT?

There are great differences among individual cats' ability to cope with stress.

- Character (genetics) plays a role. Some cats are just born with more self-confidence than others.
- If a kitten is not well socialized, he can remain more fearful and sensitive to stress his whole life.
- We know from research that the mother cat's stress or malnourishment during pregnancy can greatly affect her kittens, both in utero and over the course of their lives (various studies cited in Turner & Bateson, 2014).

ENVIRONMENTAL STRESS

A cat's environment also plays a big role. Cats are control freaks by nature. They can suffer from chronic stress if their environment is unpredictable or cannot be controlled.

Stressors outside your cat's control might include having too many cats in one house, or a dog your cat is frightened of. Many cats are afraid of babies and small children because they are completely unpredictable, whereas a cat can reasonably predict how an adult will act.

When an owner acts unpredictably—such as by punishing their cat—that is a significant source of stress. Cats can also be sensitive to tension in a household, such as frequent arguments or an in-progress divorce. A cat who does not get much rest will also become stressed out—for example, if she is constantly woken up to cuddle.

HOW CAN YOU TELL IF A CAT IS STRESSED?

Cats are not that good at showing stress. They're rather inclined to go to sleep or retreat to a quiet spot. There is nothing wrong with that, but if your cat holes up in the attic for much of the day or only dares to use the litterbox at night, that is a big problem.

Some signals of stress have been mentioned already, like yawning (see page 25) or excessive grooming (see page 29).

STRESS LICKING

Owners often don't recognize the so-called *stress lick*: The cat swallows and then quickly licks his lips. Similar to "tongue flicks" by dogs, this is a clear stress signal (but of course, not if the cat has just swallowed a tasty morsel)!

OTHER SIGNALS OF STRESS

- Anxiously pacing back and forth, not wanting to lie down, constant vigilance.
- Rippling skin.
- Playing less.
- Loss or increase of appetite.
- Spraying.
- Obsessively chasing his tail.
- In extreme cases, a cat can engage in self-harm, biting his tail or fur or overgrooming to the point of drawing blood.

The stress lick

Each of these signals can also indicate a medical issue. When in doubt, please check with your veterinarian.

STRESS BE GONE!

If you are worried that your cat is stressed out, of course you want an immediate solution. You aren't the only one: Fighting stress in cats has become a big business. There are all kinds of anti-stress aids on the market. These are great for the manufacturers, but may well be snake oil.

IDENTIFYING THE SOURCE OF STRESS

Treating the symptoms of stress is not the solution, nor is administering anti-stress aids. Many of the products on the market have yet to be proven effective, and some may actually heighten stress, such as applying valerian drops to your cat's fur.

Before you buy all kinds of products in an attempt to restore your cat's happiness, it makes more sense to seek out the root cause of your cat's stress and tackle it. In many cases, an anti-stress aid is not needed.

BOREDOM

Boredom is a very common cause of stress-related behavior. When a cat is not sure what to do with herself, she paces through the room endlessly, bothers the other cat in the house, or (in extreme cases) develops obsessive behaviors. Her owner's first response is usually to try to calm the cat. However, the cat does not want to be calmed down; she wants to play, hunt—feel challenged. Offering more, and more varied, play and ensuring your cat gets enough physical exercise (not just puzzle toys) can be of tremendous help in relieving her stress (see page 179).

Cats want choices

If a cat had his way, he would always have choices. I don't mean you should offer him three types of food. (That would actually create stress.) A cat wants to be in control and make his own decisions, in as many situations as possible. This means not being petted too much or for too long, not being picked up against his will, not being locked up with, or having to share a litterbox with, another cat he dislikes, and many other things. While it is not always possible to give a cat these choices, this book will equip you with many ways to do so.

Offering lots of challenges and play is a good way to prevent stress

GLAD OR MAD: WHAT DOES A CAT FEEL?

For a long time, people thought that animals couldn't feel pain, let alone emotions. However, there have always been scientists who think differently about this, including Darwin. Their theories fell on deaf ears at first because they had only anecdotal proof, which is not taken seriously by the science world.

BLACK BOXES?

The concept of "emotions" in animals was still disputed in the twenty-first century, and some theorists (called "behaviorists") continue to think that animals are so-called "black boxes," in that you apply a stimulus to one side (for example, the sound of a bird) and then corresponding behavior comes out the other. The animal in question supposedly has no feelings; it is simply reacting how it is programmed to react. In the opposing camp, there are researchers like Frans de Waal, who has long been convinced and has shown in countless ways that animals do have emotions.

ANOTHER APPROACH

Another approach comes from the famous Estonian neuroscientist Jaak Panksepp. Using brain stimulation and brain scans, he showed that there are many correspondences between humans and other mammals when it comes to emotions. His favorite saying at lectures was, "We are all brothers and sisters under the skin."

THE IMPORTANCE OF RESEARCH

"How important can it be?" you might ask. "Let the academics fight it out—I already know my cat can feel happy or mad." But we shouldn't brush this kind of research aside: By learning about animals' emotions, we can better understand what they need and protect their well-being.

That is the case not just for cats and dogs, but also for agricultural animals like chickens, cows, and pigs.

MALICE OR MISUNDERSTANDING?

Research into animals' emotions is therefore very important—but this topic remains problematic because we actually know very little about it. Also, we humans are inclined to wrongly interpret animals' emotions by projecting our own feelings onto them. How often do you hear that a cat did something deliberately to "annoy" his owner? This idea can lead to unnecessary punishment and stress.

PRIMARY AND SECONDARY EMOTIONS

There are different ways to name or categorize emotions, but people most often distinguish between *primary* and *secondary* emotions.

Primary emotions originate from the "old" part of the brain, so called because it evolved first. It is similar in humans and many animals. The primary emotions include fear, anger, and lust, and they are necessary for survival. In short, lust leads to offspring, fear steers you away from danger, and anger helps you defend your territory. For many scientists, it's no longer up for debate that animals do have these primary emotions.

It gets trickier with secondary emotions. These originate in the "higher" part of the brain, or the part that developed much later in evolution. Examples of secondary emotions include jealousy and guilt. They require a certain degree of reflection, of being able to compare your own situation with that of another. Whether animals can do this, and, if so, to what degree, is still very difficult to prove. So, as of now, many researchers assume that animals do not have secondary emotions.

It is not impossible that research will someday prove that they do.

Now, let's take a closer look at jealousy and guilt.

JEALOUSY

As an animal that was originally solitary, a cat is programmed to serve its own interests. What we perceive as "jealousy" often has to do with resources like food, water, a place to sleep, or the owner's attention. Does your cat join you when you are sitting on the couch with your baby? Maybe this is the only time you've sat still all day. Didn't you always used to snuggle your cat when she came to sit next to you? Cats adore attention and want to return to their trusted routine. If one cat comes running when you give another cat a treat, it is not because he doesn't want her to have the treat. He knows there is a good chance he will get something yummy as well. Jealousy has nothing to do with it!

GUILT

Guilt is another emotion we still know nothing about, as it has never been studied in cats. But guilt in dogs has been the subject of interesting research. Alexandra Horowitz found in her 2009 study that dogs act "guilty" when scolded by their owner—but the real question is whether they truly felt guilty or anxious. Dogs who had not "stolen" a biscuit reacted with greater intensity than the dogs who had. According to the researchers, this was because the dogs had no idea why they were being scolded, adding to their nervousness.

Can dogs feel guilty?

In a well-constructed follow-up study (Ostojić, 2015), dogs were given a chance to eat a treat off a table out of their owners' view. There were four scenarios: When a dog ate the treat, the researchers either did or did not replace it, and when a dog did not eat the treat, the researchers either did or did not remove it. The owners then returned to the room and observed the dogs' behavior. Each owner was then asked whether they thought the dog had eaten the treat, or whether the researcher had removed it.

The researchers thought that if the dogs really did feel or show guilt, the owners would be able to tell which dogs were "guilty" from their animals' behavior. As it turns out, no matter what their dogs had done, the owners could not tell. Their answers were no more accurate than you would expect based on coincidence. More research is always needed, but this does cast a different light on animals' feeling guilt.

A cat is certainly no dog, but I imagine the results would be no different with cats.

THE PERSONALITY OF A CAT

Every cat owner knows it: Each cat has his own unique character. Yet, there has been surprisingly little research into cats' personalities. Rather, stress and the factors that cause it have always received a lot of attention. The comparative lack of focus on personality is strange, because of course a cat's character determines *how* she experiences her environment.

WHAT IS PERSONALITY?

Personality is defined as "individual differences in patterns of behavior that are relatively stable over time and in different situations." For instance, the cat who is always first to investigate new objects in the house will also do more exploring in the yard.

ORIGINS OF PERSONALITY

A cat's personality originates in kittenhood and probably even before then. It is a complex process involving genetic factors and experience, as well as her environment. Unfortunately, the precise role of each of these is still largely unclear.

We know from research that the father's genes have a big impact on the character of his offspring (McCune, 1995; Turner, 1986). Needless to say, the mother also makes a genetic contribution, but it is more difficult to distinguish between what she passes on through her genes and what by upbringing. At animal shelters, for example, anxious mother cats are often separated from their kittens relatively quickly so the kittens don't adopt their mother's fearful behavior.

Environment also plays a crucial role. Kittens who are handled by different people while young respond differently to humans than do kittens who were only found at 12 weeks old. Negative experiences make a big impression on kittens, and that can affect their relationships with people for life.

EMERGENCE OF PERSONALITY

Once a cat's character has developed, it probably remains constant for the rest of the cat's life. Feline personality traits have only been studied in animals one year or older, but kittens already exhibit differences in temperament, such as their level of activity (Raihani, 2014). These individual differences remain stable during their first month of life. More research is needed to see if they do in fact stay consistent after this period.

Overactive kittens are sometimes spayed or neutered early in the hopes they will calm down. If their behavior is due to their personality, however, sterilizing them will not make a difference.

COAT COLOR AND PERSONALITY

For years, people have tried to establish a scientific link between the color of a cat's coat and personality. So far, not a single study has confirmed this connection, but ideas about the relationship between a cat's color and her temperament are very difficult to dispel. This has to do with a psychological principle called "confirmation bias." That is, we are inclined to pay attention only to those things that confirm our opinions.

"Torties" have an unfounded reputation for being strong-willed

Suppose a tortoiseshell cat is acting aggressively on the veterinarian's table. People can be quick to think "typical tortie" and file this away in their memory ("See, that's how they are"). If the cat is calm, however, they don't notice anything out of the ordinary. Ultimately, we remember whatever confirms our own opinion, while other events are ignored or forgotten. Thus, our misconceptions—in this case, the "tortitude" stigma—persist.

HOW INTELLIGENT ARE CATS?

Are cats intelligent? Are they smarter than dogs or not? As an owner, naturally you want your own cat to be the smartest animal in the world. Maybe you secretly hope that cats are smarter (*much* smarter) than dogs. But we shouldn't foreground the question of feline intelligence, because all cats need to do, by nature, is *be* cats—and they do that quite well. Any other expectation is a projection of our own desires.

AS SMART AS A FISH?

Every animal plays a role in the ecosystem and is best equipped to perform that function. A cat can climb a tree; a fish cannot. That does not mean that a fish is less intelligent than a cat. A popular aphorism applies well here: "If you judge a fish by its ability to climb a tree, it will live its whole life believing that it is stupid."

DIFFICULT CATS

There has been a great deal more research into canine behavior and intelligence than feline. Dogs are easier to study than cats, as they are used to working together with humans and performing tasks for us, whereas cats are not. So, scientists know comparatively little about cats' intelligence.

Another problem lies in designing intelligence tests that fit the natural behavior of a cat. It is questionable whether some of the existing research actually measured intelligence, or something else.

CAN A CAT COUNT?

The Persian cat Cuty Boy from Dubai has become famous on the internet. According to his owners, not only can he count; he can multiply, divide, and understand the Pythagorean theorem! A study (Pisa, 2009) did find that cats can learn to distinguish between a picture of two dots or three, but when the researchers enlarged the two dots so that their combined size equaled that of the three dots, the cats could no longer tell the difference. The owners of Cuty Boy are exaggerating, I'm afraid. But in any case, how would counting abilities help a cat to survive?

OBJECT PERMANENCE

If an object disappears from view, that doesn't mean it's gone. Cats understand this, which is known as having "object permanence." If you toss a cat toy behind a pillow, your cat will look for it there. This type of intelligence serves a cat's natural needs—after all, she has to remember which hole the mouse disappeared into.

Cats also have good spatial memory. In other words, a cat can remember quite well where she last found or did not find food. This is a quintessential feline trait, as well. On her daily rounds of her territory, she knows exactly where the mouse holes are. If you move your cat's food bowl but she keeps going back to where it was, that does not mean your cat is dumb. She just has a good memory!

Various experiments have shown that cats perform well when they can "be themselves."

CAN A CAT LEARN?

A cat knows what his food dish and litterbox are for. He knows that the sound of a certain car means you're home. There are cats who can run an entire obstacle course like a dog can. Other cats teach themselves to open a door. Even smarter cats train their owners to open the door when they plop themselves in front of it. So, a cat can indeed learn things. (There is a more detailed discussion of learning further along on page 143.)

A CAT'S MEMORY

Some cat owners think a cat cannot remember anything longer than one minute (or 30 seconds), but learning is impossible without memory.

Memory can be divided into two categories (to phrase it simply): short-term memory and long-term memory.

SHORT-TERM MEMORY

Short-term memory is also called *working memory*. Working memory has limited capacity and can only remember something briefly: You need to remember a phone number only until you dial it.

The length of cats' working memory has been studied by making them wait a short time before they can look for an object that has been hidden. Researchers found that cats have a working memory of about 60 seconds, but after the first 30 seconds they do worse and worse. A mouse is probably already gone by then, so that makes sense.

LONG-TERM MEMORY

No research has been conducted into cats' long-term memory, so we do not know with confidence how long a cat remembers. But, if you bring the cat carrier down from the attic after a year, your cat immediately knows to hide under the bed. And some cats recognize their brother or sister after a year.

How long a cat remembers also has to do with the intensity of a past experience. Both humans and animals find it difficult to forget a very impactful event.

A GOOD START: SOCIALIZATION

To a cat, a human is just another type of animal, one she must learn to interact with. If you have a sociable, purring cat at home, you might think human interaction comes naturally. That is often true, but it is worth considering the complex underlying process.

WHAT IS SOCIALIZATION?

The first eight weeks of life are very important to a kitten. The period between three and (roughly) eight weeks is called the *socialization* or *sensitive* period, because a kitten is particularly open to new experiences during that window. This is rather special, given that all animals have an innate fear of new things, which makes sense because "new" means "potentially dangerous"—and being able to identify danger can make the difference between life and death.

A kitten's fear is temporarily suppressed so he can discover all kinds of important things. But around the age of eight or nine weeks, his fear of unfamiliar things begins to slowly ramp back up. Again, this makes sense, because around this time, a kitten starts venturing farther and farther from the litter, greatly increasing his chance of dangerous encounters.

In this socialization period, a kitten learns to identify and interact with other cats. He also becomes familiar with other stimuli in and around his litter, so it's important for different people to pick up the kitten regularly, to familiarize him with the idea of humans.

This is also the period of social play. During play, kittens learn social behavior toward each other and where the boundaries of play are. Cats who grow up without littermates may display "play aggression," biting or scratching their owner or other cats in the family.

Social play peaks at about eight to nine weeks, and extends until approximately 14 weeks. From 14 weeks on, when kittens play together, it more and more often ends in a brawl.

Unfortunately, not enough research has been conducted into the socialization of cats. We do know that kittens develop physically more quickly (for instance, their eyes open earlier) and are less scared of strangers if picked up by different people when young. If a kitten has missed out on something during the socialization period (like meeting humans or dogs), she still can learn to interact with people. However, the older the kitten is, the slower the learning process.

THE RIGHT START

Kittens develop more quickly when handled from early on

A responsible breeder will ensure that kittens are introduced in good time to everything they will encounter later—especially people, children included. Ideally a kitten will also be introduced to dogs, vacuum cleaners, cars, and all kinds of other things before being adopted.

FERAL KITTENS

Animal shelters regularly receive kittens who have been found on the street or in the woods. Don't be reluctant to bring such a kitten home. It should be no problem at all: A feral kitten who is raised in a foster home will become just as socially agreeable as a kitten born in a home.

Only if a kitten has not seen any humans during her first eight to nine weeks is there a chance that she will remain frightened of unexpected noises or movements. This can also happen with purebred kittens left too long in a separate room without being able to participate in the household. (Some people worry that these frightened cats have been abused, but that is not necessarily the case.)

A good start:
early exposure
to other animals

10

HOW DO I CHOOSE A CAT?

Choosing a new cat is always exciting. Once you start looking, it's hard not to fall for their sweet faces, soft fur, and the funny (or heart-wrenching) stories you might read about a cat on the internet. In this section, I'll discuss how to choose a cat when you don't have any other cats in your home.

PROPER PREPARATION

This may sound counterintuitive, but it's not always the best idea to "follow your heart" when selecting a cat. To ensure a happy life together, you'll want to consider your choice wisely.

Essential questions to ask

- What kind of cat do I want? (Affectionate? Curious? Playful . . . or do I want a "lap cat"?)
- What do I have to offer a cat? (Lots of peace and quiet, or a busy family? A small studio, or a single-family home? Do I have time for a cat, and so on?)
- Which cat fits this scenario?

Answering these questions before you start looking will help you find the ideal cat for you!

A KITTEN OR A MATURE CAT?

KITTEN

Who can resist such an itty-bitty ball of fur? However, a kitten might not be the best choice for everyone.

- Kittens are bursting with energy and grow up quickly. Today's little cutie can turn your home upside-down by tomorrow. If you are attached to your designer furniture or costly antiques, a kitten might not be such a good idea.

- If you are often away from home, it is best not to adopt a kitten (or even an adult cat, for that matter).

- With a kitten, you'll have to wait some time for her personality to emerge. If you're lucky, a good breeder or shelter can often tell you something about it, but usually you won't have much information to go on.

- A kitten has a lot to learn, and raising one demands time and energy. This won't be possible if you don't have any left to give!

ADULT CAT

If you opt for an adult cat, you will have a better idea of who you're bringing home:

- The history of rehomed cats is generally known.

- Adult cats are (typically) a bit calmer.

- Because kittens are more likely to be adopted, you'll have more cats to choose from when considering adults (including young adults).

CONSIDER ADOPTING AN ELDERLY CAT!

Because cats are living longer and longer lives, a seven- or eight-year-old animal is actually just halfway: She still has some great years ahead of her. Cats at her age can still be rather playful, too. They are not necessarily layabouts.

Elderly cats have a hard time at shelters because they do not adapt as easily and may not be accustomed to having other cats around. They are often passed over in favor of younger animals who are more quickly adopted. When you take an older cat home, you are giving him a fantastic new lease on life. "Seniors" are very loveable and will have no trouble winning you over.

Is it better to adopt one or two cats?

Adopting two kittens, or placing a kitten with another young, playful, social cat is preferable for a good start.

A kitten who grows up without other cats is much more likely to be bored and display "problem behaviors" like play aggression: scratching and biting during playtime. And don't forget that once your kitten grows up without a playmate, you can never add another cat (or dog)!

WHEN CAN A KITTEN LEAVE ITS MOTHER?

The age of separation is crucial because when a kitten is taken from the litter too young, he has a greater chance of behavioral problems. And contrary to popular belief, it is definitely not true that a kitten who can eat independently is ready to be taken from the litter.

In the US, many states set the legal minimum age to separate a kitten from her mother at eight weeks, and a few states set it as low as six weeks. See www.alleycat.org/kittenprogression for guidance on telling a kitten's age.

Safe and sound with mom

You'll see big personality differences even within the same breed—or litter

That said, this minimum age is still not the best time for a kitten to be adopted. I would recommend waiting until the kitten is at least 10 to 12 weeks old. But, if she is in a situation that is harmful or even dangerous to her, of course it's better to take her away and bring her to a safe home.

MALE OR FEMALE?

Actually, this doesn't matter! Some say that male cats are more affectionate, but the differences between individuals are so great that character is really more important than gender. Two practical considerations are that it is more expensive to spay a female cat than to neuter a male one, and male cats generally need more space in the house than female cats do.

A SHELTER CAT . . .

Shelter cats unfortunately have a bad reputation with some people, who fear there must be "something wrong" with them. Most of these cats, however, are perfectly normal, sweet individuals who were stranded by their owner's death, divorce, or other personal circumstances.

By the way, you can occasionally find even purebred cats at a shelter!

CHARACTER

These days, many shelters use the Meet Your Match Feline-ality Adoption Program: Cats are tested for character, and potential owners answer questions about their expectations of a cat. Better matches are made, and many fewer cats are returned in disappointment.

BEHAVIORAL PROBLEMS?

Only a small percentage of shelter cats exhibit behavioral problems—and those that do are not necessarily "difficult" cats, or incompatible with you. For instance, a cat who is scared of small children and behaved aggressively out of fear might very well be the perfect housemate for a quiet couple.

. . . OR A PUREBRED?

Although many owners are happy with a "simple" housecat, others want nothing other than a pedigree cat—because they like the look of a particular breed, or they have experience with that breed and so can better predict what the new cat will be like. Indeed, an advantage of purebred cats is that the animal's character is fairly well understood. For instance, Siamese cats are said to be social and extroverted, Norwegian Forest Cats independent, and Ragdolls calm and gentle. A responsible breeder will give you information about the animal's lineage, too. Do keep in mind, however, that the character differences between two individuals of the same breed can be great.

BEHAVIOR

Before you adopt any particular breed, be sure you're informed of any special needs or traits typical of the breed. For instance, Savannahs and Bengals are very popular because they are so beautiful, but these cats should come with an instruction manual, as they are very active and demand a lot of attention.

HEALTH PROBLEMS?

Some breeds have inherited diseases or health problems due to their genetics or physical traits. Persians and Exotic Shorthairs, known for their short noses, have associated respiratory problems. Also, these cats almost always have chronic eye and dental problems. The Scottish Fold has a genetic mutation that affects the development of cartilage to thank for its "cute" folded ears. This means the cat already has osteoarthritis at a young age, and the pain that comes with it. These are just a couple of many known examples, showing how important these considerations are when choosing a purebred cat.

PEOPLE CATS

Finally, if you are opting for a purebred and want a cat to cuddle, look for a breed that especially loves people (rather than preferring other cats). True "people cats" include Somalis, Abyssinians, Rexes, and Sphynxes.

Should you separate cats or kittens from each other?

If you want only one cat or kitten, never take one from a duo who are very attached to each other. There is an ample choice of other cats who would rather live solo!

What could be better than playing with your brother?

PART 2
The cat and other cats

A CAT'S TERRITORY

Territory is hugely important for cats—we call them "territorial" for good reason. But a cat's idea of "territory" is different than you might think . . .

RANGE

First of all, there is a difference between a cat's territory and his "home range." (Note, though, that some scientists, books, and studies use these two terms interchangeably.)

In the wild, a cat's home range is wherever he hunts and wanders around; it is bigger than his territory. The size is determined by the amount of available food. For tomcats, the presence of female cats also factors in: During breeding season, tomcats venture out farther and more often, expanding their range. There can be overlap between the home ranges of cats (including male cats).

TERRITORY

The territory is smaller: It is the part of the home range where a cat sleeps, eats, and, in the case of female cats, nurses kittens. Cats (fiercely) defend it against invaders.

Cats' territories do not usually overlap, but female cats who live in a group often share their territories with each other.

TERRITORIAL OR NOT?

How territorial a cat is is partially determined by genetics. Savannahs, Bengals, and Norwegian Forest Cats are a bit more territorial than other breeds. Hormones factor in for cats who aren't spayed or neutered: When female cats are in heat, there are more fights than otherwise. Fights are also more common in the center of the territory than on the periphery.

The feline population keeps increasing, which means more frequent encounters between outdoor cats. Fights can happen indoors, too—for example, if an unfamiliar cat walks through your cat door uninvited. A cat's territory does not follow the borders of our gardens and patios; their boundaries intersect ours.

For indoor cats, home range and territory are one and the same (by necessity). Indoor tomcats need more space than females do, even after they are neutered.

TIME-SHARING

A cat usually has clear preferences for places to sleep or sit, although these preferences can change suddenly. Cats who cohabit will engage in time-sharing to prevent tension and make life easier. One cat might sleep on the bed during the day, while another sleeps there at night. Or one sits on the living-room windowsill in the morning, while the other takes the afternoon shift. Cats will not readily change this arrangement if it is working out well.

You can help your cats by distributing food, water, litterboxes, and sleeping places throughout your home so they have a choice of where to eat or sleep.

PATROLLING AND MARKING

Territory is crucial to cats. That's why they want to patrol their turf a few times a day to make sure everything's still okay (and nothing out of the ordinary has happened while they were looking the other way).

Why do cats sometimes sit in front of a closed door and meow?

It can be really nerve-racking for your cat when you block her ability to patrol her territory, for example, by shutting a door. That's why your cat will sometimes sit in front of a closed door meowing, yet make not the slightest move to pass through the door when you open it for her. By opening the door, you give your cat freedom of choice again, and that's her number one top priority.

PATROLLING...

When a cat goes on patrol, he checks on the smells in his territory. Has another cat passed by? Is there enough of his own scent left? He will spray over the scent of another cat to cover it up. There may even be reason to add some new scent markings.

...AND MARKING

Cats leave their mark:

- by rubbing against objects with their lips, cheeks, or tails. The black, oily substance you find on doorjambs or windowsills is the waxy excretion from their scent glands.

- by spraying. Cats who have not been neutered mainly spray either to attract a mate or to mark territory. (Female cats spray, too!) It's more complicated with sterilized cats, whose spraying can be marking behavior or a reaction to a stressful situation.

- by leaving droppings. This is apparently less about smell and more about visibility. The poop is left prominently in the middle of a field or lawn to make a statement.

A cat likes to mark corners and things that stick out

Left: Scratching leaves visible traces for other cats

Right: Marking

- by scratching objects. This is a way to catch two birds with one stone. By scratching, cats transfer their scent *and* leave a visible signal for other feline passers-by. You'll often see cats sniffing scratch marks on a tree trunk.

Do cats mark the perimeters of their territory?

Cats don't mark the outer perimeters of their territory; they mark places that are important to them. These might be protruding branches, corners of tables or fences, passageways through hedges, doorjambs, et cetera. A cat likes to follow set paths, both through her own territory and when she goes out hunting. She also marks the intersections of those paths.

NICE AND SAFE

Kittens are born deaf and blind, so the smell of the nest is vital to them. Researchers think the smell of the nest has a calming, stress-relieving effect on kittens. Adult cats also like to surround themselves with their own scent. You'll see that timid cats rub their heads on furniture more often than self-assured ones do. A cat may also suddenly start marking more indoors in response to tension between cats, or in fear of an unfamiliar cat outside. Doing so means he encounters his own smell all around him, which makes him feel safe (or safer, anyway).

LIKE A PERFUME SHOP?

Consider your cat's sensitive nose in your home. Cleaners containing chlorine or bleach are an invitation for her to urinate or spray over the smell. (It is therefore not a good idea to use these to mop your kitchen.) Be conservative with air fresheners and fragrances like incense. To a cat's sensitive nose, it's as if she just stepped into a perfume store, and you're certainly not doing her any favors.

The safe smell of the nest

Don't put anything aromatic like valerian drops or scented collars on cats themselves. Your cat can't groom away these foreign fragrances, which usually leads to stress.

HUMAN OR HOME?

We used to think that a cat was more attached to his territory than to his owner. We now know that isn't true. There are plenty of cats who go on vacation with their owners, or who move multiple times without problems.

How deep is the bond between cat and owner? This depends in part on your cat's character, but you, the owner, also have a big role. If you play with your kitten frequently, and continue even when she has grown up, you will maintain a strong bond. The same goes if you have two cats, by the way—some people worry that a cat with a feline playmate "won't want anything to do with me anymore," but the more you engage with your cats, the better your relationship will be.

WHAT DO CATS THINK OF OTHER CATS?

Is a cat a social animal—or not? The research is still out on a definitive answer—but we are learning more and more about relationships between cats.

THE CAT WHO WALKED BY HIMSELF

There is one thing we know for sure: Cats originated as solitary animals who increasingly started living in groups under the influence of humans. With the exception of lions, all members of the cat family (*Felidae*) were initially thought to be solitary. But recently, evidence is mounting that some big cats interact and cooperate with each other more than we assumed. That said, we still don't know to what extent.

A cat doesn't depend on other cats for her existence. In other words, she is not "social by necessity." A cat is social by choice, and not all cats want to be. Some cats can get along with another cat just fine, but others would much rather stay alone.

MOTHER CATS AND GROUPS OF CATS

A lot of research has been done into the social structures of farm cats and feral cats. Cats live in "matrilinear" groups, i.e., mother cats keep their daughters with them. In addition, they all (plus any other female cats in the group) take care of the kittens—even going so far as to help each other through labor and nurse each other's kittens.

So, families of female cats form groups—from grandmas to granddaughters, and including aunts and nieces (MacDonald et al., 1978, 2000). A female cat may leave the group if there isn't enough food, but this is not often the case. Young males, by contrast, are pushed out of the group at about six months old. At first, they will form their own groups for mutual safety and support—but as they become better able to fend for themselves, they will gradually disperse. Most adult males are "loners"!

BIG DIFFERENCES BETWEEN CATS

In evolutionary terms, you could say that cats are in a transitional phase between being a solitary species and a social one. There are big differences between individual cats in terms of their need for contact, both with people and with other cats. The most important factors are genetics (innate disposition) and socialization.

It is not just the mother cat who plays a role in her kittens' character. Despite his being out of the picture almost all of the time, we know from research that a social, friendly male cat fathers social, friendly kittens (McCune, 1995; Turner, 1986).

Socialization also plays a crucial role: Cats who have grown up with other cats and continue to live with others—whether purebreds at the breeder's or ferals in a colony—are generally very social toward other cats because they have learned to get along from the time they were kittens. But even among these cats, you'll find individuals who would much rather live alone.

HOME ALONE?

Many domestic cats live in one-cat households, or at least start their home lives that way when they are adopted solo as kittens. When such a cat becomes older and less playful, some owners think they should get a kitten to keep him company. Often that doesn't turn out so well, because their cat is absolutely unaccustomed to living with other cats. The result is a bored kitten because she can't play with the other cat, and an older cat who doesn't dare come down from the attic. For both cats, this means at best tolerating each other their entire lives, but never really living happily ever after.

This problem can carry on for "generations" of cats, because when it comes down to it, the kitten is growing up alone as well and won't be able to get used to another cat either.

3

MAKING FRIENDS:
A GOOD MATCH BETWEEN CATS

Adding another cat to your household is not as simple as you might think. It will only be a success if the new cat is a good match with your current cat.

ANOTHER CAT IN THE MIX

There are two reasons why we want to have another cat: for ourselves (because you have fallen in love with a photo on a website, because you want to give a poor cat a good home, or because your current cat is less affectionate than you had hoped) or for your cat ("maybe she feels lonely and would like to have a playmate"). But in practice, bringing home a new cat or kitten is not always the success we hope for.

When two cats in the same household don't make friends, we comfort ourselves by saying, "Well, as long as they don't fight." But we wouldn't be happy living with someone we don't like! As far as I'm concerned, cats shouldn't have to either.

Ask yourself critically why you want an additional cat or kitten, because your current cat is almost never actually asking for one. (If your cat has lost an established companion, see Mourning, page 78.)

Siamese cats are social with other cats

When is it better not to adopt another cat?

- If your cat has lived alone for many years or grew up without other cats.
- If you already have a stable group of cats, even just two. There is a very big chance that a new cat will disturb the equilibrium.
- If there is already tension in your home. (Complex strategies where the new cat is supposed to befriend Cat X to divert her attention away from the strife between Cat Y and Cat Z don't work out.)
- If your older cat has dementia or illness, or is deaf. Stress often leads to additional symptoms of illness; let him enjoy his old age in peace.

A GOOD MATCH

A good match with the cat or the kitten you already have is the first step on the way to harmonious cohabitation.

There aren't any foolproof rules for a "good match" because every cat is different. However, there are some basic principles that can guide you to a good choice.

SHOULD YOU ADOPT ANOTHER KITTEN OR AN ADULT CAT?

- A kitten shouldn't be your default choice. Contrary to what is often said, a kitten is not necessarily easier for your older cat to accept: While it's true that kittens adapt well to new situations, older cats are not exactly eager for a little ball of energy to join the household. You won't be the first owner whose shell-shocked older cat retreats to the attic in misery.

- If you have an older cat living alone, it is better to adopt two kittens who can keep each other busy. (But why would you want to stress out your current cat in his old age?)

- If your adult or elderly cat is truly lonely (see the box on page 80), consider adopting another adult cat who is social toward others. The character of the new cat should be compatible with your cat.

- It is fine to add one kitten to another kitten or young adult.

A cat is almost never asking for another cat

A good match

- When choosing a kitten as a playmate for another cat, don't adopt the kitten who comes up to you first. This does not mean the kitten has "chosen" you, but rather that she's a bold little cat who's very human-oriented. This isn't necessarily the ideal personality to introduce to another cat.

THE GENDER OF THE OTHER CAT

When choosing a new housemate for your cat, character is paramount. Nevertheless, some people overemphasize gender, saying it's better to adopt a female if you have a male and vice versa. That advice is not based on the natural behavior of cats: They actually live in groups of just females or just males (see page 62).

When choosing two kittens from a litter or from a group of kittens, the kittens' character and need for play are the decisive factors. Males often play more aggressively than females do and, in that respect, can be a bit too much for shy female cats. Having said this, if two kittens in a nest are best buddies, of course you will want to adopt them together, regardless of their gender or character.

DOES PEDIGREE MATTER TO CATS?

Purebred cats can be placed together with ordinary cats, and cats of different breeds can also live together just fine. However, there are some factors to consider:

- Cats of the same breed are often drawn to each other, so if one cat is different he may be excluded from the group.

- The greater the difference between two cats' activity needs, the smaller the chance that they will get along. Athletic Bengals, for example, are unlikely to live comfortably with couch-potato Persians or British Shorthairs.

- Some breeds are mainly human oriented; others are more drawn to socialize with other cats. Many so-called Eastern breeds (for example, Siamese, Oriental Shorthairs) and those with Asian blood (Ragdolls, Birmans, and Persians) fall into this latter category. A combination of a cat-oriented Eastern breed with a human-oriented breed like an Abyssinian doesn't always work out so well, even if they appear to be related.

- Breeds that tend to be somewhat more territorial than others, such as Bengals, Norwegian Forest Cats, and Savannahs, don't always want to share their house with other cats.

Each cat has his own character

The differences between breeds can be great, but so can the differences between individual cats within one breed—so you should take a good look at the character of the cat you have your eyes on. Not every cat fits the popular image of his breed!

"BUT HE WAS SO FOND OF HIS SISTER"

Bearing in mind that every cat is an individual makes clear that you can't just "replace" one cat with another. An owner will say, "He was so fond of his sister, but now he is afraid of the new cat!" That's logical, because the busy new kitten is not his gentle, shy sister. A cat can really dislike Cat X but get along just fine with Cat Y!

Unless your cat is clearly grieving for his lost companion, he is seldom asking for a new housemate (especially one he can't pick out). Be understanding if his initial reaction is fearful, or even hostile.

Purebred cats are usually well-socialized with other cats. For that reason, breeders will often say that you can just go ahead and place the cat with other cats without any "introduction." But you should be careful about this: Even if your new purebred is very social, the cat you have at home might feel differently. Always opt for a gradual introduction; it's much less likely to go awry.

INTRODUCING A NEW CAT

Cats should only be introduced with patience and diplomacy. You might encounter a breeder, neighbor, or internet commentor who says otherwise—but they never seem to have a solution when things really go south!

REASONS TO INTRODUCE THE CATS TO EACH OTHER:

- If their first encounter is negative, you'll have a big problem on your hands. It takes a long time and a lot of effort to coax frightened or aggressive cats into a harmonious group. In many cases, it will never succeed, and you and your cats will live to regret it.

- Once a fight has begun, it is not in cats' nature to surrender; they will never give in. You'll end up with one cat afraid for his life, and a relationship that can never really be repaired. So never let cats "fight it out"!

TAKE THE TIME YOU NEED

It does take a little while to introduce a new cat calmly, but ultimately it reduces stress for everyone (yourself included).

Be understanding of the fact that your cat must suddenly share her territory (and your attention), and let her set the pace. If she is receptive to the new cat, you can go through the following step-by-step plan and bring them together fairly quickly—maybe even after one or two days, especially if they are still kittens. But if she is very distrustful, take your time going through each step.

You can use this plan if you are bringing home a second cat, and also if you have multiple cats to introduce to one another.

STEP 1: GIVE THE NEW CAT HIS OWN SPACE

The introduction will be the easiest if you give the new cat his own closed-off space, such as the attic or a guest room, with everything he needs: food and water, a litterbox, a scratching post, and toys. First, check the room carefully for any escape routes. Also, don't give him your own cat's favorite room; she won't appreciate being "banned," even if it's temporary.

STEP 2: EXCHANGE SCENTS

Take two socks or washcloths and rub one against the cheek of each cat, then put it in the other cat's room. Reward each cat when he or she comes near the sock. Don't go any further if either cat has a negative reaction to the other's scent. If either cat hisses or growls when they smell the sock, you'll want to tackle the next steps more slowly. But if each seems completely uninterested in the other's scent, you can proceed directly to Step 3.

STEP 3: EXPLORING THE HOUSE

Carefully allow your new cat to explore his new house: Keep your resident cat enclosed in a separate room, or use the time when she is taking a stroll outside. Open the door to your new cat's room, and let him go exploring at his own speed. After he returns to his room, your other cat can discover that the newcomer has been out and about. Here, too, you'll determine how quickly to follow the next steps, based on how the cats react. It can take a few days to a week before they are at ease again.

STEP 4: SEEING EACH OTHER

The most delicate phase is when the cats see each other. The crucial thing during this step is to keep the cats as far apart as possible!

- Start with each cat in their own room. For example, prop the newcomer's door open slightly while the other cat is in the hallway. Keep the door from opening all the way with a hook so you are certain that they cannot get at each other.

- Find a strategic place for yourself, so you can shut the door immediately if tension arises. You can give both cats a treat. (This is most easily done with two people, one to keep an eye on each cat.) Shut the door if there's any growling, but a bit of hissing won't hurt.

An introduction can sometimes take a few weeks. Don't rush!

- Prevent the cats from running toward each other, using a treat or maybe a toy to distract them. You might find it challenging to keep a new kitten from approaching your resident cat. (Be sure to give your kitten plenty of playtime before you set up an encounter.)

- Make sure the cats see each other only briefly, to avoid anything unpleasant happening. This can be for a few seconds, maybe a minute— but no longer than that if it's the first time.

- If tensions rise, close the door again (put the newcomer back in his room), and distract each cat with a toy. Try it again later, or the next day.

- Be careful: The longer the encounter, the greater chance it will go wrong! It's better to arrange five brief meetings over the course of a day than have one long meeting with upset cats at the end. Aim to end every encounter on a positive note!

STEP 5: EXPAND

Continue as above, leaving the cats in each other's field of vision longer and longer. At a certain point, they may walk up to each other and sniff each other. Always stay with them so you can calmly distract them if necessary, and be ready to separate them safely if tensions rise. Keep a firm piece of cardboard, large tray, or big towel on hand so you can quickly block their view of each other. Make sure each cat has a good escape route.

This is the phase that will take the most time. Don't be disappointed if it takes longer than expected . . . Cats can't be forced to do anything!

If your cats become a bit used to each other but still can't be in the same room without supervision, then a screen or a gate is a good idea— for example, between the living room and hallway if that's where they spend their time. This way, they can see each other and become accustomed in their own time. Don't do this yet if the cats immediately run toward each other or stare at each other.

Dos

- Do keep encounters brief (don't let tension escalate between your cats).
- When cats stare at each other, it can turn into aggression. Interrupt staring by distracting the cats with a toy. If that doesn't help, calmly separate them.
- Make sure there are abundant escape routes in your house: high shelves and other hiding places where your cats can keep a distance from each other. The more they can make their own choices, the easier the introduction will go.

Don'ts

- An obsolete recommendation is to rub each cat with the other's scent. Don't do this, because your cat has no choice in the matter. Would you start thinking more kindly of your neighbor if you had to smell his aftershave all day?
- Don't force the cats to eat together. Even if they do so without fighting, it doesn't mean they like it. (But you can use treats to reward the cats in each other's presence.)
- Using a cat carrier during the introduction often doesn't work— but a large crate may be a different story if your cat has enough space in it. Only try this if your cat feels comfortable in the crate, and cover part of the crate with a blanket so your cat can hide out.
- Don't use a squirt bottle to spray your cats with water or yell at them if things don't turn out how you had hoped and they start fighting. This causes extra stress. There are other ways to separate fighting cats, such as throwing a towel over them.
- Don't make your cats change rooms too often. If they are moved every few hours, that is very stressful—and unconducive to a positive experience.
- Above all, try avert to any catfights! The more often they fight, the smaller the chance your cats will ever get along.

Keep meetings brief; don't let the tension mount

IF AT FIRST YOU DON'T SUCCEED . . .

Sometimes an introduction does not go as planned—usually because the owner went through the steps too quickly, before their cats were ready to proceed. The best approach here is to start from scratch.

Separate your cats once again for at least 48 hours when there has been a fight (longer if their stress level is high). Your cats must not be able to see each other. Once they are fully relaxed, you can try the step-by-step plan anew.

AND IF YOU STILL DON'T SUCCEED?

Your pet's well-being comes first. Don't condemn her to a life of stress due to the presence of another cat. Keep in the back of your mind that, in some cases, it's better to part with the newcomer—no matter how cute a kitten he might be. If you have used the plan above and your cats have not made any progress toward a friendly relationship after a few weeks, this is probably the best solution for everyone.

Curious about the new kitten

Right: The aim of any introduction is for the cats to become true friends

5

BODY LANGUAGE IN GROUPS

We humans are not always great at interpreting our cats' body language (as discussed earlier) . . . but we are often even worse at reading the dynamics between cats. We don't always pick up on tension that can make it stressful for cats to live together.

NO FIGHTING BUT STRESS ALL THE SAME

The fact that two cats don't fight doesn't mean there isn't any stress between them. You can draw a parallel with how we operate as people: You might find one of your officemates or a neighbor annoying, but you probably won't start a screaming match with them. Nonetheless, you can be under significant stress when you bump into that neighbor, or when that annoying coworker makes *another* weird remark. Ultimately you may stop enjoying your work or your home.

Cats who always kee their dista or lie with backs to ea other aren friends

Should I let my cats fight it out?

A cat's vocabulary does not include "I surrender." Fighting cats will keep at it until one seizes an opportunity to escape, or to the death. That's obviously not a good prospect for a cat, so she will try whatever it takes to avoid a fight. If the cats in your home are fighting, they have crossed a boundary, and the relationship is severely damaged. Mending it will take time and effort.

That's why I never recommend leaving cats to "fight it out." You'll usually end up with one frightened cat whose scared body language only elicits more aggression. Your best course when there's an (impending) fight is to intervene by distracting the cats. Don't yell; instead, clap your hands, or make some other neutral noise. If your cats are so intent on fighting that they cannot be distracted, throw a towel over them to break it up. The objective isn't to punish your cats—it's to interrupt the fight!

A GOOD OBSERVER

We can watch cats' body language to understand the relationships between them—but it's easy for us to overlook or misinterpret the subtle signals that more than suffice for cats.

Friends?

- Real friends groom each other regularly, go looking for one another, play together, and lie or sleep nestled together, often facing each other.
- True friends share each other's beds, litterboxes, and other items.
- Cats who never lie down together don't care for each other. They may lie down on the same couch, but if there is always distance between them, and their backs are usually turned, then they are clearly not friends.

SUBTLE HINTS

- Cats try to avoid aggression by averting their eyes and looking away. Since they can't stay out of each other's way inside the house, they use this avoidance tactic to act as if the other cat isn't there.

- Staring is always a precursor to aggression! Cats may stare at each other intensely, but this can also be much more subtle. Take the cat who walks unsuspectingly into the living room, finds a staring cat, and does a quick about-face—his owner might not even notice.

- Some assertive cats will sit conspicuously in a doorway, on the stairs, or in front of the litterbox so that the other cat doesn't dare walk by (anymore).

Staring
precedes
aggressi

MASKED INTENTIONS

- Some cats are covert operators: They will get in a bed or on the couch with another cat and then turn in circles or stretch out as intrusively as possible until the first cat runs away. Or, they start licking the first cat profusely, with the same result. It's not necessarily a problem if this happens now and then—but it *is* a problem if it's always the same cat being chased from his favorite spot.

- Sometimes you'll see one cat pounce on another cat's back and bite her neck. This isn't actually a sign of dominance (or that the first cat wasn't properly spayed or neutered); instead, this is usually an invitation to play.

Never close two cats who don't get along into one room!

PLAYING OR FIGHTING?

You can tell the difference between play and aggression by paying attention to the following points:

- Playing is always quiet (at least vocally). Growling or hissing is not part of play.

- Cats' claws are not out when they play.

- Cats may bite during play, but this is gentle.

- Cats take turns initiating play.

- If a cat disappears right after "playing" to hide in a corner, then it wasn't really play.

- Playing cats often have a "play face," with their mouth half-open.

- Cats who don't like each other will never play together.

- Play is never preceded by staring.

It is easy to tell when kittens are playing together: They will take turns pushing each other down and running away, only to turn right around and continue playing. "Threatening" poses, bushy tails, and walking sideways are all part of the game, not signs of aggression.

Kittens playing

MOURNING

A cat who loses a housemate can be quite upset. (This can happen even between cats who could not stand the sight of each other in life.) There are also heartbreaking stories of cats who literally waste away after their owner has died. It seems that cats do indeed grieve, even though there has been little to no research about this.

DO ALL CATS GRIEVE?

Not all cats grieve. If two cats had a strained relationship, the one left behind may be relieved to have her own space to live in unharassed, even if she looks around for the deceased cat and seems upset for a few days. This more likely indicates stress (due to the radical change in her household) than true mourning.

The cats who mourn do so to varying degrees (which also goes for people, by the way). Some are really thrown off their game, and for quite some time; while others just fine again, soon enough. A study by the US Humane Society (Schulz, 1996) found that 65 percent of cats exhibited multiple behavioral changes after the death of a feline housemate.

HOW DO YOU RECOGNIZE BEREAVEMENT IN CATS?

THE MOST COMMON BEHAVIORAL CHANGES ARE . . .

- increased meowing
- sleeping more
- eating less
- acting more needy toward the owner
- searching for the cat who has "vanished"

AND SOMETIMES ALSO . . .

- spraying
- staring into the distance
- not wanting to play

HOW LONG DOES GRIEVING LAST?

One individual is so different from the next that there's no predicting how long a given cat will be bereaved. But we *can* observe behavioral changes—from "none at all" (the relieved cat) to changes lasting a few days, or even months. Research by the Humane Society found that even the most intensely bereaved animals stopped showing behavioral changes after six months.

DO CATS NEED TO SAY GOODBYE?

Does it help the surviving cat to "say goodbye"? Outcomes here can vary greatly, and thorough research is still lacking. Some cats don't react to the body of their deceased friend, others really do say goodbye—and still others panic at the sight. This is especially likely if their companion was put to sleep by the vet and brought back home. Such a cat smells different, and in some cases the surviving cat will not recognize her anymore.

What if you can't let your other cat say goodbye? Don't feel guilty! Sometimes it simply isn't possible, and that is not the end of the world.

HELPING A GRIEVING CAT

Routines are important to a cat. By continuing your daily activities as much as possible, you'll send your cat a calming signal. If your cat wants more attention, give it to him. He is not feeling well and needs support and comfort.

If you don't already play with your cat at set times, this is a good reason to begin (see page 178). Even if your cat doesn't feel like playing, bring out a bouncer wand, string, or ball at the same time every day. Eventually she'll join in! There is no better way to get over sadness and listlessness than to play together.

How can I tell if my cat is lonely?

This is the big question after one cat dies: Is the left-behind cat lonely, and how can I tell? The answer lies in good observation. In any case, don't immediately adopt a new cat. Give your "lonely" cat ample time to adjust, and see if he picks up his old routines.

- If your cat perks up and flourishes, let him stay alone!
- Wanting to play a lot and other attention-seeking behavior does not necessarily indicate loneliness. It can also mean that your cat has more space now than she did before. You yourself will also likely be inclined to play and cuddle more with your surviving cat, which may make it seem that she is seeking more attention.
- If your cat seems in danger of wasting away—for example, if he really doesn't want to eat, play, or cuddle—it is a good idea to adopt another cat. This especially applies to social breeds (see page 54) and cats who were inseparable from their former companions.

DOMINANT CATS?

Many people are convinced that it's a feline practice to establish "dominance." For example, they say that a cat is being dominant if she "tackles" or bites your arm. Perching in high places, pooping in the house, coming to join you when you call a different cat or are busy with the baby—these are all supposedly signs of dominance. I recently even read someone's claim that purring means a cat has accepted her subordinate position.

WHAT IS DOMINANCE?

Because so many different behaviors are called "dominant," it's clear that cat owners lack a collective idea of what exactly dominance is: It has something to do with wanting to be the boss, but what? I've had owners tell me that one cat is very dominant, and add in the next breath that he always sits and watches as his sister eats all the food from his dish.

Animals who live in groups regularly have little standoffs and flare-ups with each other. If the outcome of these contests is always the same—in other words, the same individual always "wins"—a hierarchy develops in the group. Animal A is dominant over B, B over all the others minus A, and so on. Even two individuals can have such a hierarchy.

The advantage of a hierarchy is that the members don't have to fight over food and other important things all the time, since it has already been established who gets to eat first, for example. But one's place in this kind of hierarchy is set: The same cat can't be dominant one minute and surrender his food to another cat the next.

DO CATS HAVE A PECKING ORDER?

Given the solitary origin of cats, it is illogical to suppose that they have a hierarchy. True, cats today do live with other cats—but it's going too far to say that cats have now become a totally social species.

When the famous cat researcher John Bradshaw took a fresh look at all the studies on feline dominance, he showed that their conclusions were not supported by the data. He also found no indications of dominance in his own study (Bradshaw, 2003).

NOT SUBMISSIVE

If cats don't have a pecking order, then they don't need to fight to establish one. What is more, cats try to avoid fights as much as possible. A cat who sometimes takes a swipe at another cat is not dominant; he might just not feel like having the other one around.

If cats don't display "dominant" behavior, then naturally "submissive" behavior is also a misnomer. A cat lying on her back is not really "submissive"—nor is a cat with her tail between her legs.

BEING THE BOSS OF YOUR CAT?

The misperception that we have to be "the boss" of our pets has been hard to get rid of. Unfortunately, there are still owners who try to be "more dominant" than their cats. Some will push a cat to the ground or (physically) intimidate her in other ways if she does something she isn't supposed to. This doesn't solve anything; it is only likely to cause aggression or fear.

THE BOSSY CAT

If there is no pecking order among cats, hierarchical dominance becomes moot, but what about cats who act "bossy"? It's true that some cats are more dominating by character—I prefer to call them "assertive" because "dominant" has such negative connotations—but here, too, the term is used much too quickly. Look at things from a cat's perspective, and many behaviors can be explained in a different way.

A cat who always takes the first turn at the food dish might just have a bigger appetite than the other cat. The first one in the cardboard box or at the door? This cat is probably more curious or has a greater need for challenge. Pooping in the house usually means there's a problem with the

litterbox (see page 94); biting your arm can be playful or aggressive.

Of course there are those cats who are truly more assertive and like to hog the food dish or all the space in the cat bed. You may need to intervene, but don't punish your assertive cat. She can't change her character!

PART 3

The cat in the house

ON TOP OF THE WORLD!

A cat doesn't need to live in a huge castle to be happy, but keeping eight cats in a one-room apartment isn't a good idea either.

HOW MUCH SPACE DOES A CAT NEED?

The general rule is not to have more cats than rooms (where the cats are allowed). In other words, according to this rule, if your cat is allowed in the living room and nowhere else, you should limit yourself to one cat, regardless of the size of the rest of the house. If she can go into the living room and kitchen, then two cats are the maximum.

This may seem unduly conservative, but cats want to be able to hide out without having to see other cats. Plus, it's best to have enough space to distribute food dishes and litterboxes throughout the house, so your cats can access these without running into each other if they don't want to: This prevents conflicts. If there is already tension, it is especially important that your cats can stay out of each other's way.

ON THE LOOKOUT

Cats like to have an overview of their surroundings. The best lookout posts are up high, in any case above their other housemates. Cats are real control freaks: Your cat wants to keep an eye on everything. Plus, as an animal who prefers flight to fight, he wants to be able to see "the enemy" coming in time. That enemy can take many forms, from another household cat who frightens him, to the children with their little grabby hands.

That's why it's a good plan to have perches your cat can climb to. You'll expand the your cat's living area, especially if your home is small. If you have multiple cats, you can create peace and space with perches. Plus, the chance to climb is a positive challenge for your cat.

ON TOP OF THE WORLD

Your choice of climbing trees is huge, from traditional cat furniture made from carpet and sisal rope, to sleek new designs. Many cat trees offer a combination of climbing and scratching. If you don't like the way such furniture looks in your interior, you can attach shelves along the wall so your cat can walk from one side of the room to the other without touching the floor. You will find lots of inspiration on the internet if you are considering some DIY!

WHAT SHOULD YOU CONSIDER WHEN BUYING CAT FURNITURE?

- The product must be sturdy, with no danger of breaking apart or falling over. DIY shelves on the wall should ideally be covered in fabric or carpet so your cat doesn't slip and fall when jumping up or down.

- Distance: The distance between the shelves or the "landings" of a cat tree shouldn't be too big. Your cat should be easily able to jump from one shelf to the next. Young cats climb effortlessly, but your elderly cat will still want to access his safe spot.

- Space: If you have multiple cats, arrange your cat tree or your DIY design in such a way that one cat can never force another into a corner or otherwise block her escape route. In other words, there always have to be two "exits."

Why are cats sometimes afraid to come back down?

Right: Getting down is a bit harder than getting up!

Cats are skilled, enthusiastic climbers. Their claws, which curve inward, are primarily useful when the cat is climbing *up*. When he wants to get back down, his claws don't help him in the same way. That's why some cats slowly descend backward, so they have some grip. Other cats jump down—but that's not possible if they have climbed too high.

SCRATCHING, OR: HOW DO I KEEP MY FURNITURE IN ONE PIECE?

A cat cannot go without something to scratch in the house, even if she scratches trees and fences when outside. Scratching is a natural and necessary behavior for your cat; you can't train her not to scratch. Luckily, you can divert her scratching from undesirable places to acceptable places, such as her scratching post.

SCRATCHING AND SCENT-MARKING

A cat has multiple reasons to scratch: The top two are to maintain his claws and to leave his scent behind. He does this both for himself and to leave a sign for other cats.

Enthusiastic cleaners who keep wiping off scent markings in the house (those black traces on doorframes, for instance) may motivate nervous, uncertain cats to mark them over and over again. That is why it is so important to have a scratching post in the house: It gives your cat at least one set place where he can leave his scent time and time again.

TENSION AND EXCITEMENT

Scratching helps your cat stretch her muscles, for instance when she has just woken up. It can also be an outlet for tension or frustration, as well as positive energy. You might have a cat who never scratches the furniture except when you come home after being away all day. She's happy to see you! When your cats have been playing together and are still full of adrenaline, they may suddenly hang on to the scratching post (or your couch).

If there is a fight or tension between the cats in your group, they might scratch the furniture or scratching post even more. Watch to see whether one of your cats hangs conspicuously from the scratching post when another cat is close by. This can indicate that there is tension under the surface.

ATTENTION SEEKING

Finally, scratching can be a way to get your attention. It's a rare owner who doesn't mind if their cat scratches the furniture or wallpaper. The best way for your cat to get your attention is to run purposefully up to the couch the second you walk into the room. If you don't respond right away, an outstretched paw or claw on the couch is usually enough to really get your attention.

THE RIGHT SCRATCHING POST

Scratching posts come in countless sizes and designs. Your choice of a post (or an entire climbing castle) should be based on what works for your cat. It's the only way to protect your furniture or wallpaper from your cat's claws!

Here are the most important tips for choosing the right scratching post and the best place in the house to put it.

HORIZONTAL OR VERTICAL SCRATCHING?

There are cats who only scratch horizontally (on mats or the couch seats) and there are vertical scratchers (walls, climbing posts, trees). That's an important consideration when buying a cat scratcher, because a cat who scratches horizontally isn't very likely to use a post. Instead, you can satisfy these cats with rough mats (like ones made of coconut fiber).

Some cats are "horizontal scratchers"

SURFACE MATERIAL

- Many scratching posts are made with sisal rope. It's most often wrapped horizontally, but many cats actually prefer to have the cord/grain running lengthwise—one possible reason why your cat does not use his post.

- Some cats prefer to scratch cardboard or paper. These are the cats who have a good time scratching the wallpaper. There are countless cardboard scratchers on the market, from simple ones to attractive (expensive) designs.
- There are also cats who prefer to scratch (bare) wood. There are now scratching posts for them as well, although of course you can often find a piece of (natural) wood yourself.

STABILITY

A scratching post has to be sturdy and not fall over even if the cat hangs from it. That cute little 20-inch-high kitten post with the funny ball hanging at the top won't really suffice once your cat is an adult, because he can knock it over with one claw. Then he'll go for the couch or Grandma's antique chair instead because they are quite a bit more stable. If you buy flat scratching boards, attach them firmly to the wall or floor.

On the lookout

STRETCHING

Cats like to stretch out as they scratch. Scratching posts and boards should be tall enough that your cat's claws can't reach past the top when she stretches.

THE RIGHT PLACE

Large cat scratchers are usually placed in a corner of the room, but that's not great for your cat because he would like to have something to scratch along his most-frequented route. You can also supplement your large cat tree with other posts or boards elsewhere in the house.

A cat wants to stretch out fully when scratching

- Put multiple scratching options on or next to walking paths.

- Consider exits and entrances (doors) because cats like to mark when they come inside from outside.

- Consider the area where your cat sleeps, so she can stretch on a scratching post when she wakes up.

- You cat needs something to scratch where she regularly is—not (just) in the cat room, but also in the living room. A cat who wakes up in the living room isn't really going to walk through the rain to the tree in the yard before stretching out.

- With a group of cats, you have to take into account their various preferences for surface material. Here again, it's important to create multiple scratching places in the house, to prevent stress.

DIY CAT SCRATCHERS

If your budget is tight or you don't like the look of carpeted scratchers, you can make them yourself. This can include coconut mats affixed to the wall, cork tiles stuck onto a stable surface, a door or piece of furniture covered with carpet, and so on. You can find all kinds of great suggestions on the internet. Don't use materials you already have in the house, because your cat won't be able to tell the difference between that piece of carpet you hung up especially for her and your new floor rug.

TRAINING CATS NOT TO SCRATCH FURNITURE

What should you do if your cat completely ignores his perfectly good scratching posts?

First check whether the scratching options meet the requirements above: They're in the right place, the right size, and well designed. If so, then use the following plan:

- First offer an alternative for scratching.

- Make the furniture or wallpaper unappealing.

- Reward your cat when he uses the scratching post.

A cat always needs something to scratch!

FIRST OFFER AN ALTERNATIVE

- Put a scratching post, board, or tree immediately next to where your cat scratches now, so she nearly stumbles over the scratcher when she walks to the couch.

- You can enhance the appeal of the scratching post by spraying it with valerian or catnip, if your cat likes either scent.

MAKE FURNITURE OR WALLPAPER UNAPPEALING

- Put a couch cover or a large sheet over the chair or couch that's being scratched (affix it firmly on the bottom so your cat can't crawl underneath)! The smoother the covering, the less attractive to your cat.

- Alternatively, if your cat limits herself to a small area of your furniture, you can cover it with a piece of thick (adhesive) plastic film or special "anti-scratch" double-sided tape like Sticky Paws.

- Note that many cats find aluminum foil very fun, so it is not a universal repellent.

REWARD YOUR CAT WHEN HE USES THE SCRATCHING POST

At first you can reward him when he walks up to the scratching post. Then in the next phase, only reward him when he has used the scratching post.

It might be inconvenient having the scratching post right next to your couch. Once your cat is using it well, you can move it bit by bit to a better place. Only then should you remove the sheet or tape from the couch.

COMMON MISTAKES

- Don't allow your cat to continue scratching an old couch or chair because "when we get a new couch, I'll train her not to." Once your cat has been scratching furniture for years and is accustomed to it, it is virtually impossible to train her to stop.

- Don't substitute your old, worn-out scratching post with a new one overnight. First, put the new one next to the old one so your cat can get used to it gradually.

SAY NO TO DECLAWING

Declawing involves more than just removing your cat's nails: It's actually an orthopedic surgery that amputates the end bones of your cat's toes. This surgery involves general anesthesia and requires pain management before, during, and after. Despite how complex declawing is, there are no standard guidelines for the process, and not every cat receives the necessary pain treatment.

Cats are digitigrades, meaning they stand or walk on their digits (toes). It doesn't take much imagination to see why this would make declawing extra-painful for your cat.

The consequences of declawing are profound. Cats can experience pain for the rest of their lives; putting weight on their limbs can hurt; and they can also develop chronic back pain. And since cats are very good at hiding pain, you might not even realize that your cat is suffering.

Declawed cats are also more at risk for behavioral problems like peeing and pooping outside the litterbox, biting, and aggression (Martell-Moran, 2018). These issues arise when pain stops a cat from performing her natural behaviors: no stretching after a good nap, no scratching to express excitement, and no marking when feeling threatened by other cats.

Declawing is prohibited in most parts of the world, and in some countries it's seen as animal cruelty. Although this practice is quite common in the US, it's becoming more controversial: More and more US states are now banning declawing.

There's lots of advice in this book to prevent your cat from shredding your furniture without the need for invasive surgery. Happy cats need their claws!

You can buy
scratching furniture
in every size, shape,
and material

CAT IN THE BOX:
ALL ABOUT THE LITTERBOX

If your cat could talk, no doubt he would tell you how important his litterbox is to him. Most of all he wants a clean litterbox, but there are also a few other requirements. A litterbox that's dirty, not easily accessible, or otherwise unpleasant is a source of stress—what's more, it's also bad for your cat's health. Did you know that a cat who holds in his pee until he dares to use the litterbox has a greater chance of developing a urinary tract infection? The following tips are certain to please your cat (and will prevent him from peeing elsewhere in the house).

SIZE

A cat must be able to turn around easily in his box, so choose a litterbox that is 1.5 times as long as your cat (from nose to tail). If your cat is still growing, check regularly to see if his litterbox is still big enough.

APPEARANCE

- Some cats who like to hide out prefer a covered litterbox; others would rather be able to look around. You can try out both to see what your cat likes; many boxes come with an optional added top.

- Every cat dislikes the door flaps in some litterbox covers, even if they do still use the litterbox (by necessity). These doors keep the odor in the litterbox and can make your cat feel cooped up. For older cats, a door can cause pain or irritation if it falls right on their back. Do you find the litterbox needs a door to keep from stinking? Then it isn't clean enough!

- There are top-entry litterboxes on the market that a cat has to jump up on before entering. These may seem like a good idea because your cat will track less litter out of the box. But this style is not advisable for older cats or if there are tensions in a group of cats. The cat inside may feel threatened if another cat suddenly stands over the entrance.

- Don't choose a litterbox with a grate the cat has to stand on. Furthermore, cats don't like plastic bags or newspapers lining the bottom either.

HOW MANY LITTERBOXES?

- By nature, cats prefer to use different locations to pee and poop. Even if you have only one cat, you might need two boxes, especially if your cat pees and poops outside of the box. Preferably, these litterboxes should not be next to each other.

- If you have multiple cats, the recommendation is to have one litterbox for each social group, plus one extra. Theoretically, cats who form a social group (who are good friends) don't mind sharing a litterbox. Still, you should always provide one extra box so the cats can have a choice.

- If you adopt a new cat or kitten, the newcomer must have her own litterbox. If the cats get along well with each other, you can take the extra box away later on.

CLEAN, CLEANER, CLEANEST

- Cats are very clean animals by nature. Thanks to their sensitive noses, they also smell left-behind urine much better than we do and will be put off sooner. Scoop the kitty litter at least daily, not just for poop, but also urine. Clumping litter is great in this regard; it lets you remove urine much more easily than does non-clumping litter.

- Besides scooping, you need to clean the litterbox regularly: Ideally you should do this once a week. You can use hot water and a gentle cleanser like dish soap. Do not use strong-smelling, harsh detergents or bleach.

- Once you have washed the litter trays thoroughly and left them to dry, it's a good idea to change the litter. I recommend using your nose: When in doubt . . . use fresh litter!

- Of course, you should always carefully wash your hands after you have been in contact with the litterbox. This also protects you from the parasite *toxoplasma gondii* that can infect cats and appear in their poop. If you are pregnant or immunocompromised, it's best to delegate litterbox duties, if possible, to avoid the (small) chance of contracting toxoplasmosis.

- If the litterbox is kept clean, you won't need any extra deodorizers. Cats also really dislike air fresheners in or near their litterbox, which can be a reason a cat might start looking for an alternative location.

A QUIET SPOT

- Pick a quiet spot for the litterbox where your cat can safely retreat. It's better not to put it in a room that's very busy or has a lot of foot traffic. (This is especially important if you have small children.) Also, don't put it next to the washer or dryer; your cat can get scared if a machine makes a sudden noise while he's in the litterbox.

- Cats like to have an overview of their surroundings while in the litterbox. So, it's better not to position a covered box with its entrance facing a wall.

- Don't put litterboxes in cupboards or other built-in structures. Dark, isolated places (basements or sheds) are not a good idea either. The more difficult it is to reach the litterbox, the lower the cat's motivation to go—plus, you might forget to clean the litterbox.

- If you have multiple cats and therefore multiple litterboxes, distribute the boxes throughout the house, one on each floor, for example.

- Young kittens can get so busy playing that they forget they have to go. For these little kitties, put a litterbox (or an extra tray) wherever they spend the most time, so they can get to it quickly.

- The distance to the litterbox can also become a problem for older cats. If your cat has arthritis, he probably thinks the basement is too far to go.

KITTY LITTER

Today, there is a huge selection of different types of kitty litter. The most important thing is that your cat does well with the type you choose. Unfortunately, you can't always tell if your cat is really happy with his litter, even if he does use the litterbox.

Cats who don't cover their poop or pee usually don't like their kitty litter. Scratching on the sides or outside of the box can also indicate that your cat isn't too thrilled with your choice of litter.

Your cat may also try to avoid her litterbox by holding her pee.

WHAT YOUR CAT LIKES

- Cats are desert animals by origin. The more kitty litter resembles sand, the better your cat will like it. Choose litter that has as fine a structure as possible. Wood pellets, ever so popular these days, do not meet this requirement and often cause cats to do their business outside the box!

- Clumping litter is convenient mainly for you, so you can quickly scoop the litterbox and leave only clean litter behind. However, don't use clumping litter for young kittens, as they may ingest it while playing in or around the litter tray, which can obstruct the kitten's little stomach. You can switch to clumping litter once they are about five months old.

- To be environmentally conscious, you can choose litter made of paper, wood, corn, or even walnut shells. You can get clumping litter in these varieties as well.

- Choose odorless kitty litter, since cats have sensitive noses and aren't fans of additives like baby powder or citrus scent. Several brands advertise their "fresh scent," meaning that there are chemicals added. You can recognize these by the blue particles in the litter. Needless to say, these brands are no favorite of cats, either.

- Cats are creatures of habit. Once you find a litter that works well, keep buying the same kind. Your cat may go outside her box if you come home every week with a different discounted brand.

A cat hangs way out of the litterbox when it's too small or otherwise unpleasant

SELF-CLEANING LITTERBOXES

I am not a fan. Most of the self-cleaning boxes I've seen are much too small on the inside for an adult cat to sit comfortably. And although these boxes don't start cleaning until the cat has stepped out, your cat might turn back to dig or sniff. If the motor turns on right then, your cat can get quite a fright and no longer dare to use her box.

My cat does fine in her litterbox. Do I still need to read this section?

Cats are fairly tolerant about using their litterboxes: I've seen cats pee in a litterbox that I thought looked too dirty to come near, and others wobbling on their wood pellets. Cats don't have a choice or don't know anything else, and so they use the box they have. Unfortunately, you can't tell from the outside whether your cats are happy with their litterbox. Research has shown that a large percentage of cats will continue to use their box even if their favorite litter is replaced with something they find unpleasant, but in that case they poop and pee less frequently to avoid their box (McGowan, 2017), which, in turn, can lead to stress and bladder problems.

Cats like to dig in something that's soft

DOES A CAT HAVE TO HAVE A LITTERBOX?

The answer to that question is brief: Yes, always! A litterbox is essential if you want to keep an eye on your cat's health. If your indoor-outdoor cat does all her business outside, you won't be able to see whether she is only urinating in small amounts, which is one indication that she might have a uniary tract infection. Your cat could be in pain unnecessarily, and there is a good chance that you wouldn't discover the problem until it's already (almost) too late. You also won't be able to check whether your cat's poop looks normal or she has diarrhea. And if your vet wants to test a sample of your cat's urine or poop, it becomes very difficult to collect it when your cat does everything outside.

There may also be times when even indoor-outdoor cats can't be allowed outside, such as on noisy New Year's Eve or July Fourth, after a move, or if your cat is recuperating after illness or surgery. Then, if your cat is not used to a litterbox, you both have a big problem.

CAN YOU TRAIN A CAT TO USE A TOILET?

This is theoretically possible—there are cats who do it. But it is quite far removed from a cat's natural behavior, so it takes time and effort to teach a cat to use our kind of toilet (so much effort that there are special kits on the market to help you).

As far as I'm concerned, this isn't something you should strive for. A cat doesn't really like it; he can't dig before and after as he wants to. What's more, you can't check his urine and poop just like with an outdoor cat. And imagine if your cat has just peed and then slips and falls into the toilet . . .

Sniffing the litterbox first to see if it's clean!

Why do cats bury their business?

This is all about hygiene. Cats like to keep their environment clean. In nature, a cat first digs a little hole and pees or poops in it (never both). After that, he carefully buries it. Kittens also do this by nature. Once they are about four weeks old, they will instinctively start to look for a place where they can dig. If your cat stops covering his business although he has always done so before, this may indicate pain or illness.

THE CAT ROOM: THEIR OWN CASTLE?

More and more households have set aside a room just for their cats. But before you start renovating, ask yourself whether a cat really needs her own room.

A CAT ROOM OR A CASTLE?

Imagine having a cat room completely set up with towering cat trees, toys, beds, and more items that make a kitty's heart go pitter-pat. Isn't that a cat's dream? Vicky Halls, a British behavioral expert, wrote about two Siamese cats who were bored. Following her advice ("give these cats more to do"), the owners converted a room in their house into a play paradise. As it turned out, the Siamese cats were kept *so* busy that they hardly ever came out of their room. It's conceivable that this was not the well-meaning owners' desired outcome.

DON'T FORGET THE REST OF THE HOUSE

A cat room is especially nice as a fancy bonus for your cat, but don't forget he needs certain things, such as a scratching post, in the rest of your house, too. After all, he prefers to scratch where he happens to be at the time and will not walk downstairs to do it. Food, water, and the litterbox will also be too close together in a cat room that's too small.

IN THE CAT ROOM WHILE YOU'RE AWAY?

I don't see the cat room as a place to keep your cat enclosed during the day while you're working, and then at night while you're asleep. If you add up these hours (honestly!), you'll see that your cat would be shut inside that limited space for quite a long time.

It's not advisable to shut cats in regularly, especially if you have multiple cats together in one room. Even if there isn't tension between your cats, tensions can unfortunately arise when they're regularly in a limited space together.

Even a cat room can become boring

5

A DREAMY PLACE TO SLEEP

Cats can sleep in the craziest places: On the internet, you can find plenty of cats stretched out on top of a drying rack or on an impossibly narrow ledge. But most cats prefer to sleep in a somewhat more comfortable place, in the sun or by the heater if possible.

SLEEPING SAFELY

Every animal looks for a safe place to sleep, and cats are no exception. You don't want an enemy to attack while you're sleeping. Some cats prefer to sleep buried deeply under a blanket or in a cat bed. Others are totally content with a spot on the arm of the couch or the top landing of their cat tree. These cats are usually not fans of a cat bed, no matter what you try.

WARMTH

Cats love heat. There are hanging cat beds you can attach to radiators or windowsills, where your cat can sleep nice and warm in the sun. No matter what your cat chooses, make sure he has options and can move to a different place if the radiator gets "too hot to handle"!

Cats love
cardboard
boxes

PEACE AND QUIET

The appearance of a cat bed is much less important than the need for
undisturbed rest.

- Don't ever wake up your cat when she is sleeping . . . not even to pet or
  to nuzzle her beautifully warm fur!

- Agree on this with your housemates and children, as well.

- Always give your cat a place to sleep out of reach of other cats and
  people—for example, a high place (the cat tree) or her own sanctuary
  where she cannot be disturbed.

Why do cats love cardboard boxes?

Set down a cardboard box and most cats won't hesitate to jump in. A
box is something new that a cat can investigate, so it's exciting.

It can also serve a different function: Research has revealed that
cats in shelters experience less stress if they have a (cardboard) box
to retreat into. Even if your cat has no stress, he may enjoy sitting or
sleeping in a small, enclosed space. A box might seem unattractive to
us, but the cardboard works well as insulation, making the box a
warm place for your cat.

DINNERTIME!

WHAT DOES A CAT EAT?

A cat's natural diet consists of small prey such as mice, rats, and birds. Cats are "obligate carnivores," meaning meat is a biological necessity for them, and they have a high protein requirement. A cat cannot survive on plant-based (or mostly plant-based) food.

Cats can't rid themselves of toxins well, so they are especially cautious with unknown food. Your cat's sensitive nose picks up the slightest differences in the composition of her food, and she will reject new foods at first. She is not picky, but careful about her own safety.

VARIATION

To keep your kitten from becoming a picky eater, offer him a wide variety of foods from the start. If he is exposed to many different flavors and textures (of dry food and wet food), he will always recognize them later. This prevents a big hassle if your cat ever has to switch to diet food, for example.

CATCHING MICE

Cats who have to provide for themselves catch an average of 10 mice a day. This natural feeding pattern of multiple small portions over the course of the day is nothing like receiving two meals a day. You might hope your cat will adapt without too much fuss because twice a day fits your schedule, but unfortunately, it's not that simple for a cat.

THE DRAWBACKS OF TWO MEALS A DAY

Some cats are so hungry by mealtime that tensions arise, and groups of cats can fall apart completely due to the stress (and ensuing aggression) of too strict a diet.

Other cats think about food all day long: When they are finally fed, they wolf their food down so fast that they throw it back up.

Do cats get fat if food is left out all day?

Cats who were used to having food available at all times when they were kittens tend not to overeat. However, a cat who is used to set mealtimes may overeat if, suddenly, food is left out for them all day long. Cats who have previously experienced hunger, such as those who were formally feral, also lose their natural inhibition to overeat. So, be careful with sudden changes to your cat's feeding schedule, to prevent him from becoming overweight or frustrated.

HOW OFTEN SHOULD A CAT EAT?

If possible, based on your cat's appetite, it's fine to have (dry) food out all day long so the cat can choose when she wants to eat. If you need to find a compromise between two meals a day and unlimited food, I usually recommend feeding multiple times per day, such as four. This is a better fit for her natural eating behavior, but will keep your cat from snacking without limits. Automatic feeders with a timer are an excellent way to help with this.

Feeding more often than twice a day also has health benefits: In cats prone to uninary infections, the acidity of the urine remains more stable during the day. We also see chubby cats lose weight when they can eat smaller portions regularly.

WHERE TO PUT THE FOOD DISH

- A cat likes to eat without being disturbed, so choose a quiet place—preferably not right next to a doorway or anywhere there is a lot of foot traffic.

- Cats like to have a full view of their surroundings, so put your cat's food dish where he can survey the room while eating, with a wall protecting his back.

- The food dish shouldn't be next to the water bowl, as cats don't like their water to be next to their "prey" (i.e., food dish).

- It also shouldn't be next to the litterbox. (We wouldn't eat on the toilet, either!)

THE IDEAL FOOD DISH

- It should be flat and wide. Cats find it annoying if their whiskers touch the sides.

- Plastic dishes absorb odors and are difficult to keep clean in the long term, so a ceramic or stainless-steel dish is preferable.

- Ideally, wash and rinse your cat's food dish every day.

Why does my cat scratch next to her food dish?

Unfortunately, there has yet to be a study into why cats do this, but the most logical explanation is that your cat "buries" her leftovers to keep her territory clean: Even if her dish is empty, the smell of food still lingers, so she wants to "put away" her food. This digging motion is instinctual (of course, it doesn't work on the kitchen floor)!

Another possible explanation is that your cat wants to hide the smell of his food from other animals to prevent them from walking into his territory uninvited.

Unlike some other animals, cats have never actually been observed burying food and eating it later.

A kitten "burying" food

I DON'T LIKE THIS FOOD ANYMORE!

Why does a cat suddenly turn up her nose at the kibble she thought tasted just fine only yesterday? This is especially frustrating when you've just stocked up on food that was on sale.

In nature, a cat catches a variety of prey and thus automatically has a balanced diet. At home, it's quite possible that a cat who receives the same food all the time needs something different. "Fussiness" is his way of ensuring he gets a full complement of nutrients.

There may also be something entirely different going on, such as pain or illness. A cat with dental problems will approach his dish often to eat, but then spit or drop food back out because chewing is painful.

A cats who feels nauseous won't bother approaching her bowl, or will lick a bit of the sauce apathetically.

If your cat still doesn't want to eat after a day, it's best to call the vet immediately. Fatty liver disease is a real danger for cats, and it can cause them to eat even less. When a cat isn't getting enough food, the body sends fat cells to the liver to use as fuel—but cats' livers do not process fat well. The liver stores it, and will ultimately fail, which is fatal. Fortunately, fatty liver can be reversed when detected and treated promptly.

MEALTIME IN A MULTICAT HOUSEHOLD

Cats are solitary hunters, and they are solitary eaters as well. "Sharing" prey is not in their vocabulary, except when a mother cat brings food to her kittens. A cat doesn't like to eat right next to another cat. Unfortunately, we tend to put food dishes right next to each other so our cats can "enjoy" a meal together. Of course, there are some cats who will eat from the same dish or switch dishes halfway through their meal— most often these cats have grown up together. They are the exception and not the rule!

My cats often fight, but never while eating. Why not?

Do your cats not get along, or even fight sometimes, but never during meals? You can't necessarily conclude that their relationship is actually not so bad. When a cat is hungry, the motivation to eat wins out over their fear of the other cat. What's more, a cat doesn't have a choice: It's eat or go hungry. In this case, you'll often see the following signs of stress.

Relaxed
while eating

STRESS DURING EATING

A cat who is at ease while eating will sit with her belly on the ground and her tail straight back on the floor. If the food is especially yummy, the tip of her tail very slowly swishes back and forth a bit.

A CAT WHO IS STRESSED WHILE EATING MAY . . .

- remain (half) standing.
- move his ears restlessly, and nervously keep an eye on the other cats.
- take a bit of food and eat it somewhere else.
- gobble down his food and then run away as quickly as possible.
- walk away immediately after eating, instead of calmly grooming himself nearby.

In a multicat household, it's best to put food dishes in several different places so each cat can choose where she wants to eat. If some locations go totally unused, you can retire them after a few days. By giving your cats options, you'll prevent unnecessary tension. There's no need to worry that your cats will grow apart if they eat in separate rooms.

DIFFERENT EATING REQUIREMENTS

Cats in the same household can have different diet needs: One cat might "graze" on little bites all day long and stay naturally lean, while another doesn't know when to stop if there is always food available. You can solve this as follows:

- Use a SureFeed Microchip Pet Feeder for the cat who nibbles all day long, and observe set mealtimes for the others. This feeder can read the ID chip your cat already has (or a special tag you put on his collar). It opens exclusively for the cat with the right chip, keeping the other cats at bay.

- As an alternative, you can put a (normal) food dish in a separate room for the "grazing" cat, and give him exclusive access using a SureFlap Microchip cat door. This works according to the same principle as above, with the benefit that he can eat in peace, without the other cats around.

- It's also possible that one of your cats eats much more quickly than the other(s)—and so gets the lion's share of the food. In this case, you can put the speed eater's portion in a puzzle feeder (see page 188), and possibly in a different room. With a bit of luck, both your cats will finish at the same time.

OBSESSED WITH FOOD

Some cats are completely obsessed with food—like the one who walks next to you if you happen to be approaching his bowl, whines and meows as you eat, or steals food from your plate.

PAST EXPERIENCE

This can be caused by a cat's past: Your cat or kitten may have suffered hunger at some point or had to fight for her food. This doesn't only apply to cats who were once feral: Timid cats who lived in a group that was too big for them, or with only one shared food dish, may not have gotten nearly enough.

Give these cats small portions regularly, possibly using a dish with a timer. This way, they'll learn to trust in regular feeding times and the behavior will probably disappear.

A food bowl that "recognizes" the right cat

ILLNESS

Another possible cause is illness. Older cats in particular may have an overactive thyroid or diabetes (see page 139), which may or may not also result in drinking more water. These cats are always hungry. So, always have your vet take a look if your cat suddenly starts eating more.

DIET

A cat on an (overly strict) diet can also develop an obsession with eating.

Why do cats bring prey home?

Popular theories about why your cat brings mice home to you include that he wants to give you a gift because he loves you so much, or he is proud that he caught something. As nice as that sounds, giving gifts is unfortunately well outside the natural behavior of a cat, and hunting (for its own sake) is instinctive, after all.

The most logical explanation is that your cat brings prey home because she feels safe there and wants to eat in peace and quiet. Cats who don't eat their catch but leave it nicely on the doormat for you probably do this because they've already had their fill, at which point they instinctively return to the center of their territory.

And why do some cats lay multiple mice or birds next to each other in a row? We're still waiting on an explanation for that one!

7

HELP, MY CAT HAS TO GO ON A DIET!

Cats love to eat, and some love it *too* much. Feline obesity is increasingly common. A fat cat is not a "cute" cat nor a happy one, since obesity is a burden on his health and well-being.

Even if your cat is not overweight, there are many other reasons he may need to switch to a prescription diet—a urinary infection, a sensitive stomach, or kidney problems, for example. Whatever the reason for your cat's new diet, you'll most likely need to be inventive and patient during the switch.

HOW DO YOU HELP A CAT LOSE WEIGHT?

If your cat is really rotund, it's best to seek personalized guidance from your veterinarian. But if your cat is just a little overweight, you can do something about that yourself. A cat loses weight in just the same way that we do: Eat less and exercise more.

LESS FOOD

Weight loss has to be gradual. Remember that a reduction of just a few grams is a lot less food, proportionately, for a cat—don't cut his portion in half.

- Either switch your cat to diet food or serve smaller portions, but don't change both at the same time.

- Recent research has shown that cats who are fed four times a day become more active, and lose weight as a result, without other changes to their diet (Deng, 2014; de Godoy, 2015).

- Dry food is very dense in calories, so cats don't need much of it, but they can feel as though they haven't eaten enough. Adding moisture to their diet, such as by serving wet food (possibly with water added) helps cats feel full without all those calories.

- Give your cat his daily portion in a puzzle feeder so he can't eat as quickly—this way he'll feel satisfied earlier on. A puzzle feeder makes your cat put some effort in to get the kibble out; this could be as simple as a ball that lets just a few pieces fall out at a time. There are lots of great options for puzzle feeders to be found online, ready made or DIY. For many cats, feeders are a fun challenge!

MORE EXERCISE

If a cat is merely given less food without more exercise, she will adapt her activity according to the calories she eats and, in the long run, she won't lose weight.

- Make sure your cat has daily play sessions that encourage her to run and jump (see page 179).
- For a change of pace, don't put your cat's food in his dish; instead, toss his kibble piece by piece around the room. This can be a fun way to increase your cat's exercise—especially in the evening, when cats are more active anyway.

TRANSITIONING TO SPECIAL DIET FOOD

There are more and more specialized foods on the market, for all kinds of situations. For many cats, switching to a different food is a considerable challenge.

- Let your cat get used to the taste of the diet food slowly by mixing some pieces in with her current food. Build up gradually. You can also do this with wet food.
- Some cats prefer the taste of wet diet food to the dry kind, so offering wet is another way to tempt your cat.
- In some cases you don't have a choice: Your cat has to switch foods right away—for example, due to a severe allergy. Try different brands and flavors: When possible, ask for samples to give your cat options. Offer each variety several times in a row, so she has a chance to get used to it. (Having something different at every meal is too confusing for a cat.)

- It's better not to offer three or four different varieties side by side. There is a big chance you cat won't be able to choose and therefore will not eat.

- Making mealtime a game by throwing the kibble across the room can also add appeal to diet food.

EXTRA TIPS FOR DIET FOOD

- Diet food is designed to meet your cat's needs, so be consistent: Don't alternate it with other (cheaper) food, and don't stop without consulting your vet.

- If your cat is already not crazy about her diet food, you should certainly not "hide" medicine in it.

- Be careful with treats: They are not harmful with some diets, but are with others. Ask your vet whether your cat can have other snacks.

Won't a cat eat it if they are hungry enough?

Unfortunately this is an enduring misconception. If your cat doesn't trust his food, he would really rather starve to death than eat his diet kibble. Waiting until your cat gives in is not an option. The longer a cat fasts, the greater chance of fatty liver disease—especially for cats who are already a bit overweight (see page 109). What's more, going hungry can actually put off your cat's appetite, making it even harder to motivate him. In extreme cases a cat can become anorexic, whereupon a vet may have to recommend forced feeding—the last thing anyone wants, especially your cat.

DIET FOOD IN A GROUP OF CATS

Putting one cat on a diet is challenging enough! If you have multiple cats and/or multiple diets, you really have a difficult situation. In some cases, you can switch your whole household to the new diet, but that isn't always possible. A kitten has to have her own food up to a certain age, for example. Other diets are so specific that they are not suitable for healthy cats.

If your cats are used to eating at fixed times, you can stand guard until everyone has eaten all of their food from the correct dish. You can also put the cat who needs special food in a different corner, or a different room, so he is not tempted by the smell of the other cats' food.

You can't suddenly switch a cat from "free feeding" on unlimited food to being fed special food twice a day. A SureFeed Microchip Pet Feeder can help in this situation. This feeder opens only for the cat with the right chip, and so your cat can graze on his new food all day long, after all.

Tummy trouble?

If the cat switching to special food has been sick to her stomach, it is best to wait until she feels better to offer the diet food, if possible. Otherwise, there is a big chance she will associate the diet food with her nausea.

Unfortunately, feline obesity is increasingly common

WATER BOWLS, FAUCETS, AND PONDS

Water is of life-or-death importance to all mammals, but many cats, in particular, drink less water than is actually good for their health.

DESERT ANIMALS

Cats originate in the North African deserts, which aren't exactly known for their large supply of water. Desert animals primarily depend on the moisture they get from eating their prey. Mice, rats, and other rodents hunted by cats are made up of 60 to 80 percent water (just like we humans, by the way).

By nature, a cat does not have a strong urge to drink. So long as she receives canned (or raw) food with a high moisture content (or lives off of prey she has caught), there's no problem. But these days, most cats are fed dry food exclusively, which goes against their nature given their origins.

A cat who eats dry food has to drink a lot of water to restore the balance. Even if you think your cat is drinking plenty, you can't tell whether your cat is drinking enough by looking at him. The difference between "too little" and "enough" is just a fraction of a fluid ounce.

The urine of cats who don't drink enough water becomes too concentrated, causing bladder problems. Kidney problems can also result, so it's important to pay extra attention to drinking!

THE IDEAL WATER BOWL

- Space the food dish and water bowl apart from each other, preferably at least six feet apart. Having the water bowl in a different place demonstrably causes cats to drink more water. This is because cats instinctively don't want to drink water that may have been contaminated by their "prey."

- Offer fresh water in multiple places around the house—for example, one bowl on each floor. Your cat will take a drink more frequently if she encounters a water bowl often.

- Choose big, wide water bowls so your cat's whiskers don't touch the sides while drinking.

- As with food dishes, stainless steel and ceramic bowls are preferable.

Why does my cat drink from faucets or puddles?

Some cats prefer to drink from the faucet, shower floor, puddles, or the dog's water bowl. I'd bet that in all these cases the cat's own food and water are right next to each other. All of these other drinking options have something else in common: The cat won't bump her whiskers when she drinks there!

You may have heard that cats think outdoor water tastes better, but whether that is really true has never been studied. Unless you live in an area with strongly chlorinated drinking water, it's not very likely. Cats always drink less from faucets or puddles when there are large water bowls in the house, and not placed next to their food.

Drinking from the faucet can mean a cat finds her bowl unappealing

MESSING AROUND WITH WATER

A cat who uses his paw when drinking may be doing this to be playful. However, his water bowl might also be too small. Another possibility is that the water level in the bowl changes too often, so the cat is just checking first with his paw.

There are cats who really mess around with their water: They jostle their bowl and lick the water from the rim, or the floor. This is often due to a bowl that's too small or too close to their food. Choose a heavy (dog) bowl made of stone or ceramic to avoid water ballet!

WATER FOUNTAINS

If you want to give your cat the royal treatment, you might consider a fountain with flowing water. For some cats, this is an amazing invention.

Remember, though, that water fountains need to be cleaned as regularly as normal bowls, and, with some brands, that can be quite a hassle. The filter also has to be replaced at set intervals.

Don't worry if a fountain isn't within your budget; multiple "ordinary" water bowls are a perfectly fine alternative!

Extra fun!

To really delight your cat, you can put a big tub or container in the bathroom or on your patio. Add water, plus some swimming robot fish toys, marbles, or some kibble to challenge your cat. This is ideal for hot summer days—your cats will be playing, cooling off, and drinking at the same time!

HOW DOES A CAT DRINK?

For a long time, scientists thought that cats drink the same way dogs do: by forming a little "spoon" with the tongue and gulping down the water. But in fact, a cat appears to have much more elegant system: She just touches the tip of her tongue to the water and then quickly retracts it. This creates a "column" of water, so to speak. When the cat immediately closes her mouth, she traps part of this column inside. Her chin stays nice and dry!

A nice, big water bowl prevents whisker stress!

OUTDOORS OR NOT?

Cats love wandering through a garden or meadow, sunbathing in the grass, and maybe even sprinting after a mouse. That is their natural behavior, but unfortunately it isn't always possible. Is an indoor cat pitiful, or can he lead a happy life?

THE OUTDOOR CAT

As beautiful as the outdoors can be for a cat, there are some lurking dangers:

- Traffic: The chance of a traffic accident is especially high for tomcats between seven and 24 months old, and more accidents happen at night than during the day. Cats are apparently streetwise: The chance goes down with every year as they get older.

- Other cats and dogs: Fights with the neighborhood cats not only cause a lot of stress, they put your cat at risk of injuries and illness (such as feline AIDS, also called FIV).

- Cat haters and bird lovers: Your cat might be abused or poisoned.

- Loss or theft: Cats (especially purebreds) can be stolen or accidentally end up in a strange house or vehicle. The more social your cat, the greater the chance that he will walk in somewhere or allow himself to be picked up by those with good or evil intentions.

CAUSING A NUISANCE

A cat who goes outdoors can cause a nuisance that seems to be less and less accepted. Particularly in neighborhoods with lots of cats (city centers!), your cat can really get in the way of other feline and human residents. Of course, it is not nice if your cat poops or sprays on your neighbor's porch, or walks into their house and eats the resident cat's food—not to mention those cats who attack other cats or dogs they

It's fun playing outdoors!

encounter. As the owner, you are responsible for your pet's conduct under all circumstances—and on the hook for the cost of any damages.

THE INDOOR CAT

Cats can have accidents inside, too, such as getting stuck in tilting windows, or falling out of a window or from the balcony. Fortunately, these are accidents you can prevent. The greatest danger to an indoor cat is the chance of obesity or behavioral problems: Indoor cats who don't have enough stimulation can become bored and may ultimately exhibit self-harming behavior (see page 36).

SO, INDOOR OR OUTDOOR?

Cats who grow up indoors will generally have no problem spending the rest of their lives inside. However, some cats have an irrepressible urge to go outside anyway: Their genes are stronger than their upbringing. It is impossible to keep these animals happy indoors.

There isn't any particular breed that's especially suited to life indoors. On the other hand, some fairly demanding breeds—such as Bengals and Savannahs—definitely require a large house, or a fenced-in yard or enclosure. Don't let these cats' beautiful appearance blind you to the fact that they need a lot of exercise and challenge!

WHEN CAN A CAT GO OUTSIDE?

- Kittens cannot go outside until they have been neutered. Female cats can already be fertile at the young age of four months. You usually won't notice when such a young cat is in heat, but unfortunately the neighborhood tomcats will notice right away.

- After moving house, the recommendation is to keep your cat indoors for six weeks. Although this isn't based on research, it's a good idea in any case to keep your cat inside for the first few weeks, so he can gradually become accustomed to his new home. You will likely let a true outdoor cat out sooner, whereas a nervous cat should preferably stay inside longer. Adequate play and other challenges will make your cat's stay inside the house more appealing while he gets situated.

FIGHTING WITH THE NEIGHBORS

Is your cat the neighborhood underdog, or the "terror cat"? Unfortunately there's no way to teach your underdog cat to "stand up for herself"—nor to reform your terror cat (or the neighbor's). Trainable moments are

Confrontations between outdoor cats are almost unavoidable

impossible when the cats are out of your control. That said, here's what you *can* do:

- If other cats are entering your house and scaring the living daylights out of your cat, eliminate this immense source of stress. An electronic door that reads your cat's ID chip is the best solution. If your cat is going into your neighbor's house, consider sharing or covering the cost of such a door so they don't get any more unwelcome visits.

- In many cases, your cat will be fighting with just one particular neighborhood cat. If you know where that cat lives, have a conversation with the owners. Propose an alternating schedule to prevent future fights—for example, allowing your cat outside during the day, and theirs at night.

- If that doesn't work, or you don't know where the terror cat lives, or your own cat continues to hassle other cats or dogs, a physical barrier is the only solution. In other words, you'll have to keep your cat inside, or find for a way for her to go outside safely.

Can you keep an outdoor cat from catching birds?

More and more people are advocating against letting cats outside because they allegedly cause tremendous harm to birds, rodents, and reptiles. Some cats even come home with multiple kills, and some manage to catch mice and birds even in their fenced-off enclosures! But, there are other cats who never catch anything. Each of the countless studies on cats' impact on the rest of nature seems to contradict the next.

Putting a bell on your cat's collar does nothing to make hunting birds less successful. As far as I'm concerned, it's best not to do this. To a cat, the jingling bell under her chin is much louder than it is to us. Also, wearing a bell means that she has to wear a collar, which can be a choking hazard. It seems more helpful to simply keep your cat inside at dawn and dusk when birds and rodents are more active.

SAFE OUTSIDE

There are multiple ways to allow your cat outdoors to safely enjoy the fresh air.

FENCING IN THE YARD

A fenced-in yard is a great alternative to roaming around outside. Your cat has some freedom, and other cats or animals cannot threaten him.

- Build your fence at least six feet high, and add netting at the top, angled 45 degrees inward.

- Another system is to attach roller bars along the top of your fence or wall. A cat trying to climb over your fence or walk along the top of your wall will lose her grip when these rollers spin. Of course, the same applies to other cats trying to get *in*. These are particularly handy in areas where many cats live. (You can find relevant products and DIY tutorials by searching for "coyote rollers" online.)

- Of course, the best solution depends on your yard, how big it is, and what it contains. A small yard with a wooden fence is easiest to seal off. High trees or hedges your cat can climb (and from there, perhaps leap right over your fence) make things a bit more difficult.

THE CAT ENCLOSURE

If you cannot fence in your yard, consider a cat enclosure or "catio." This is nothing more than a screened-in (and perhaps covered) section of your yard where your cat can safely walk around. A single cat can enjoy even a small enclosure, provided there's ample room to stretch (both standing up and lying down) and turn around. But a bigger enclosure is nicer—necessary if you have multiple cats—and they must be able to enter and exit freely. Make sure there's a cool, shady spot for the hot summer months, and ideally something for your cats to climb and scratch, even in a small catio.

If you'd rather not (or can't) have the enclosure attached to your house, you can put it somewhere else in the yard and build a covered "catwalk" to the enclosure.

THE SCREENED-IN BALCONY

Don't have a yard? A screened-in balcony is another great way to enrich your cat's life. From chicken wire to netting, there is a wide choice of materials to enclose your balcony. You can even buy screening that is almost invisible.

Always pay close attention to your cat's safety, and check carefully that he can't escape by crawling under or behind something.

An open window, carefully secured with a screen or net, can itself be pleasurable for a cat. Be careful with tilting windows: Cats get caught in these all the time. You can buy special protective grilles to prevent your cat from getting stuck in these windows.

You can enclose a balcony with netting

SHOULD YOUR CAT WEAR A COLLAR?

Collars are not necessary for cats and can even present a danger. For example, a cat can be terribly injured if she manages to worm her front leg into her collar. If you feel the need for a collar anyway, choose a safety collar that will automatically release under strain, called a breakaway collar. If you use a collar as identification, it is better to have a microchip implanted in your cat. However, some owners prefer to have their cat collared anyway, so she can easily be recognized as a pet and not a stray.

WALKING YOUR CAT?

Some cats really do enjoy taking a walk with you. There are plenty of cats who come along when the dog is let out or when their owner takes a stroll. Other cats go out on a harness.

Whether or not this is a good idea depends entirely on your cat and your surroundings. If there's a big chance that you'll encounter an unpleasant situation (dogs, boisterous or startled passers-by), of course it's better not to go walking. It also has to be fun for your cat! Unfortunately, many owners underestimate the stress a cat might experience. Nevertheless, in the right situation it isn't a bad idea to take your cat out. Is your home small, and your cat filled with chutzpah? Some cats certainly appreciate the extra adventure.

HOW TO BE WELL-PREPARED FOR AN OUTING

- It's best to start when your cat is still a kitten.
- Choose a well-fitting harness instead of a collar.
- Don't go out until your cat has become fully accustomed to the harness indoors.
- Start with short distances in a quiet area; don't look for adventure.
- Practice in the late evening or early morning when there aren't many people and dogs on the street.
- Be alert to unsafe situations—certainly not all dogs find cats charming.
- Pay close attention to your cat's body language to make sure she's having fun the whole time. A walk is meant to be fun for both of you. If in doubt, don't!

THE CAT DOOR

A cat door is just the thing if you want to give your outdoor cat more freedom, or easy access to your fenced-in yard or catio. She can go in and out when she feels like it, and you don't have to play doorman anymore.

CHOOSING A CAT DOOR

If you are thinking of buying a cat door, quality should be your first consideration. A cat who really wants to go out will easily be able to push through the latch on a cheap door.

Your cat door must also be big enough for your cat: Do you have a large breed or a cat who's a bit rotund? He wouldn't be the first cat to walk through the yard wearing his cat door around his middle!

To prevent neighboring cats from coming through the cat door for a visit, it's best to use the type that can scan your cat's microchip, such as the SureFlap Microchip Cat Door. From inside, any cat can push the flap open; from outside, only cats with approved chips can get in. (This works with the ID chip your cat already has.)

Cat doors are getting more and more advanced: The SureFlap Microchip DualScan scans cats not only when they come in, but also when they go out. This way you can keep one or more cats inside temporarily—for example, if they are sick.

To *really* keep tabs on your cats, there's the SureFlap Microchip Cat Door Connect. An app reveals each cat's exact comings and goings, and which cats are inside at a particular moment. Plus, you can lock and unlock the door with the app.

GETTING USED TO THE CAT DOOR

Most cats understand fairly quickly how a cat door works, but the following tips will help frightened cats get used to it.

- Keep the door in its open position for starters, securing it with string or tape.

- If your cat is really scared, reward him with a treat when he dares to come close to it.

- The next step is to toss a treat or piece of kibble outside, through the door. If your cat or kitten is not motivated by food but loves to play, use a string or wand toy to tempt her through the opening.

- Alternatively, stand outside yourself and encourage your cat to come through the open hatch. Repeat this until she does it without any hesitation. Reward each intermediate step—for example, when she sticks her head through the door before she's ready to go fully through.

- If this goes well, do the same from outside to inside.

- As the last step, gradually lower the door bit by bit until it is closed. If you like, you can help your cat at first by carefully opening the door when he pushes his head against it.

A "smart" cat door can be installed in a glass door, too

Some cats feel threatened when another cat sits in front of the cat door

NOT DARING TO GO OUTSIDE

The outside world itself can also be frightening. A cat who wants to go into the yard will first look around to see if the coast is clear. She feels vulnerable if she suddenly finds herself on an open patio or in a large, open yard. Flowerpots or bushes set near the cat door will give your cat some shelter before she decides to venture farther.

BARRICADING THE CAT DOOR

Once cats are used to going in and out freely, they can keep stubbornly pushing against their cat door if it is locked for whatever reason (for example, on New Year's Eve). The best way to avoid this frustration is to barricade the door by putting a wooden board or something else in front of it. If you also ignore the meowing, your cat will learn very quickly when the cat door is and isn't open.

THE CAT DOOR AS A THREAT

Although many cats will be happy to have a cat door, your cat might be among those who find it threatening. The hatch represents a gap in the defensive wall around her territory. Especially if neighboring cats occasionally stare inside through the door, it can cause stress or fear. So, it's best not to put litterboxes or food dishes near the hatch.

12

ALONE TIME, VACATIONS, AND SEPARATION ANXIETY

Can a cat be left alone, and if so, for how long? This question comes up when you're planning a vacation, or thinking of adopting a new cat. There are also owners who worry that their cat has separation anxiety.

WHAT TO DO WITH YOUR CAT DURING VACATIONS?

This is *the* biggest vacation question: What does your cat like best when you are away? The choice is usually between staying home with a sitter or boarding elsewhere. A cat generally doesn't like change. Your cat might not be thrilled to be left behind in the house for two weeks, but there is a good chance he will sleep a lot in between visits by the sitter. For many cats, especially old and anxious cats, their familiar, safe environment is the best. If you have two or more cats, they can also keep each other company and won't get bored as quickly.

CAT SITTERS

If you choose to have your cat stay at home, the next question is: Who is the best one to take care of him? Of course, it's easy to ask your neighbors or friends—and in most cases, affordable. Unfortunately, not every neighbor will be as diligent as you are with the litterbox, or stick to your feeding instructions. If your cat needs more than just routine care, or you don't want to bother your neighbors, there are professional cat sitters. They are usually more expensive, but should have

experience taking care of cats with special requirements. Always request someone's background and references before hiring them.

CAT BOARDERS

Boarding can be a good choice if your cat doesn't tend to be fearful or quickly lose heart when alone. I recommend only using kennels where your cat can have a room to himself or with his regular companions. Being placed in a large group of unfamiliar cats is too stressful for virtually all cats. Fortunately, there are more and more boarding facilities where a cat can stay alone (and to choose from, in general).

Always take a look first:

- Does the kennel look clean and well maintained?
- Do they carefully screen cats for the required vaccinations?
- How often will your cat receive attention?
- How much space will your cat have?

You can bring a cat who needs extra care, insulin injections for example, to your desired boarder for a few days on "trial." This will test whether your cat easily allows other people to give her medicine, and whether she keeps eating well.

Incidentally, your cat must always have up-to-date vaccinations before she can go to a kennel. Make sure to check the rules in advance.

HOME ALONE DURING THE DAY

Not all adult cats can deal well with being alone. A human-oriented cat *can* stay alone for several hours a day, say normal working hours, provided that you come home most evenings and build in quality time with your cat—both playtime and time for affection.

SEPARATION ANXIETY

A cat who is happy to see you when you come home from work does not necessarily have separation anxiety, even if she sits in the window waiting for you, or exuberantly rubs her head against you when you come home from vacation. There *is* a real problem, though, if a cat shows clear (physiological and/or behavioral) signs of stress when the person she is attached to is gone or out of reach (for example, behind a closed door).

To be diagnosed with separation anxiety, the cat must regularly exhibit this same behavior, and only when "their person" is gone. Cats can also develop separation anxiety around a feline companion. If you suspect your cat is suffering from separation anxiety, please turn to a professional behaviorist for help.

My cat pees on the bed or doormat when I'm gone. Is he angry?

When cats pee on the bed or a doormat while their owners are gone, this is often misunderstood as anger or fear. But the real cause may be much simpler—namely, bladder problems—so that must be ruled out first. The litterbox can also be to blame for peeing in the house: In many cases, the box is not cleaned often enough during vacations, or cats who are used to going outside must go in a litterbox instead. Cats who are punished when they urinate outside the litterbox may also "seize the opportunity" while their owner is away.

A cat who waits for you by the window doesn't necessarily have separation anxiety

THE SENIOR CAT

Our cats are living to be older and older. Sixteen years old is already fairly usual, and more and more cats are living to 20 years or beyond. According to Guinness World Records online, Creme Puff from Texas was the oldest cat ever. She lived to be 38! The average housecat won't make it to that age, but there are plenty of reasons to devote this section to the older cat.

WHAT IS CONSIDERED OLD?

International Cat Care (ICatCare.com) uses the following classification:

- Kitten: 0–6 months
- Junior: 7 months–2 years
- Prime: 3–6 years
- Adult: 7–10 years
- Senior: 11–14 years
- Geriatric: 15 years and up

Cats live longer these days thanks to the improved nutrition and medical care now available. Old age is not an illness, but aging changes the feline body, just as with people. Many of these changes go unnoticed because cats are quite good at concealing pain. Unfortunately, too many elderly cats suffer in silence because their owners don't recognize pain, or hesitate to use medication or painkillers.

The changing older cat

- A cat's iris color can change.
- His coat can become thinner, the claws thicker.
- Some cats get gray hair.
- A cat may lose weight, and she may become less agile and strong overall.
- Her senses don't function as well as they used to.

NOT THAT OLD YET!

The behavior and health of different cats in the same age bracket can vary greatly. There are plenty of cats who are still active and playful (and catch a mouse every day) at age 16, whereas other cats are already "old" at nine. Purebred cats generally don't live as long as ordinary housecats.

From about age seven, a cat may show some signs of aging. That is why your cat's annual checkup at the vet is so important—to know for sure that you haven't overlooked any problems, and so you can deal with them in time. The sooner you identify problems, the greater the chance that you'll spend many more fine years with your cat.

BEHAVIORAL CHANGES

Many changes that come with growing older are wrongly seen as behavioral problems. A cat might suddenly become grumpy or even aggressive when petted, picked up, or brushed. He may slowly become deaf, or have worsening eyesight, causing him to startle or react aggressively when he doesn't see or hear you coming. When your cat starts peeing or pooping outside the box, there's often a medical cause. A cat may suddenly have a "second childhood"—becoming extra active and licking the food dish clean or drinking a lot of water. Such a healthy appetite may not look like a problem, but in older cats it generally indicates a medical concern.

Scruffy is already fifteen

COMMON MEDICAL PROBLEMS IN OLDER CATS

ARTHRITIS

This chronic joint disease is very painful. It is estimated that 61 percent of cats older than six and 82 percent of cats older than 14 suffer from arthritis! Arthritis in cats occurs mainly in the hip, knee, elbow, and shoulder—the very joints they use to jump, as they so often do. Once a joint is affected, it's never quite the same and painkillers are needed.

Symptoms

- Playing less and sleeping more.
- Not wanting to jump up on the couch or the windowsill anymore; avoiding the stairs.
- Less grooming (particularly the back and hips) or grooming certain areas more (due to underlying pain).
- Different sleeping or sitting postures.
- Grumpiness or maybe even aggression when touched, picked up, or brushed.
- Standing while urinating (instead of crouching).
- Pooping outside the litterbox.
- Claws that click against the floor (either because your cat can't retract them any longer, due to arthritis, or because using the scratching post has become painful, resulting in less scratching and longer nails).

DEMENTIA (COGNITIVE DYSFUNCTION)

Cats can develop dementia, which closely resembles Alzheimer's in people. It's not a rare disorder: 35 to 50 percent of cats older than 15 show signs of dementia.

Symptoms

- Getting lost, especially at night.
- Walking around aimlessly or staring—at a wall, for example.
- Disrupted circadian rhythms.
- Aggression.

- Soiling the house.
- And especially: meowing at night. This is very characteristic of cats with dementia, a type of "primal scream" that seems to come from really deep down and doesn't resemble normal meowing at all. (That said, meowing at night can also be caused by high blood pressure.)

DIABETES
Diabetes occurs in overweight cats.

Symptoms

- Drinking and peeing a lot.
- Eating more but losing weight anyway.
- Restlessness.

KIDNEY PROBLEMS
Kidney problems are also common among older cats, although there is an "acute" type that can occur in young animals. The scary thing about this condition is that it only comes to light once over 70 percent of kidney function has been lost.

Symptoms

- Drinking and peeing a lot.
- Nausea, vomiting.
- Poor coat condition.

OVERACTIVE THYROID
An overactive thyroid, or hyperthyroidism, is almost always caused by a benign tumor on the thyroid. On average, cats with thyroid problems are 12 years old.

Symptoms

- Drinking and peeing a lot.
- Eating more but losing weight anyway.
- Hyperactivity (a "second childhood").
- Restlessness, sometimes aggression.
- Increased heart rate.

Essential tips for your aging cat

- When you notice behavioral changes, see the vet immediately!
- Eating or drinking more is always a reason for a checkup.
- Pay attention to your cat's weight.
- Take your cat to the vet at least once a year. This is important at every age, but especially so for the older kitty, to ensure you're providing the right diet and medication.
- Most of all, enjoy the time you have together!

HELPING YOUR OLDER CAT

All the conditions mentioned above are serious enough that your cat must be treated by a vet. Of course, also pay close attention to your cat's diet and see to it that she gets any needed medications. In addition, there are other small, practical things you can do to make your older cat's life as pleasurable as possible.

SETTING UP YOUR HOME

- Provide steps so your cat can climb up onto the couch or windowsill again.
- Put food and water bowls on a small platform so an arthritic cat doesn't need to bend his legs.
- Give your cat more comfortable places to sleep, or spoil him with a nice heating pad for his old bones.
- For a cat with dementia in particular, make the world smaller and easier to navigate by keeping her in one room. This offers security and peace.
- A cat with dementia can become disoriented, especially at night, so leave a nightlight on in the room where she sleeps. This can help prevent too much nocturnal meowing.

EATING AND DRINKING

- Older cats no longer have as keen a sense of smell, and therefore may have less interest in eating. Add some hot water to their food, or briefly microwave wet food. The heat will give the food a stronger smell.
- Make sure that your cat drinks enough, and provide multiple wide drinking bowls. If your cat drinks too little, he'll have a greater chance of kidney problems.

THE LITTERBOX

- Put the litterbox in an accessible place. Make sure your cat can step in easily (the sides are low) and that she doesn't have to climb the stairs to another floor.

- If your box has a flap in the door, remove it immediately, as a flap can cause pain or irritation if it lands right at the base of the tail. Preferably, remove the entire litterbox cover.

Cozy, accessible places to sleep are essential for a senior cat

- Consider your kitty litter: I am not a fan of wood pellets in general, but for older cats they are really a problem. These cats are less stable when standing, and can lose their balance on these hard, round pellets. Kitty litter that has a fine structure and is soft on the paws will make a big difference for your older cat.

- An older cat can sink into kitty litter that's too deep, which can also cause instability and pain when he goes in his box. Three to four inches is sufficient for him.

PLAYING

Continue to play with your cat, but don't forget she won't be able to jump as far or as athletically as she used to. It's better to have her "hunt" prey that moves across the floor (see page 192).

GROOMING

- Regularly clip your cat's claws. Because your cat moves and scratches less, her claws grow longer and can get snagged in pillows, blankets, or your own clothes.

- If you don't dare trim her nails yourself, check them regularly. A cat's claws are curved, and when they are not clipped, they can become ingrown into the soles of their feet. This is very painful of course, and can lead to severe infections.

- Care for your cat's fur in places he can't reach anymore. Use soft brushes so as not to hurt him—and, in fact, he may really enjoy this!

PART 4

Interacting with your cat

HOW A CAT LEARNS

Naturally, a cat can learn things—just like any animal—because learning is of life-or-death importance. Suppose your cat encounters a big, aggressive dog and manages to escape in the nick of time. To put it mildly, it wouldn't be helpful if she didn't learn anything, and therefore didn't run away from her next such encounter. Cats recognize the sound of the refrigerator door opening; they know how to distinguish between their owner's car and the neighbor's, and so on. Cats certainly learn things—but how do they do it, exactly?

INSTINCT

Part of a cat's behavior is instinctive. Instinct is already there at birth, and learning doesn't come into it. At about four weeks old, kittens instinctively look for some sand or soil they can dig a hole in, to make their first attempts at peeing and pooping independently. Instinctive behaviors arise on their own at the proper time, but do need some refinement by way of practice. Bird parents, for example, know they must feed a hatchling, but only gain true agility by doing it.

PRACTICE MAKES PERFECT

Young animals are curious and can get up to shenanigans. Through play, they explore their surroundings and hone their motor skills at the same time. You don't become a good climber until you've climbed a tree and fallen out once or twice (or more). By playing and experimenting, animals discover for themselves whether something works or offers any benefit. This is also called *trial and error*.

OBSERVATION

A quick and especially safe way to learn something new is to closely observe other animals doing it. Kittens learn new behaviors by watching their mother. For example, they learn to interact with people more easily if there is a calm, relaxed mother cat around.

In one study, kittens who had to push a lever to receive food learned this very quickly when they saw their mother do it first. Without her example, they didn't learn it at all (Chesler, 1969). The kittens also learned to do this sooner by watching their mother than by observing an unknown adult cat.

Mom is not the only example-setter for kittens. There is the case of one orphaned kitten who grew up with dogs. Just like the dogs, it would pee against trees, with one leg raised.

Kittens learn more readily when their mother is present

Adult cats also learn from (watching) other cats. There are countless stories of cats who start drinking from a faucet after seeing another cat do it, or who "teach" each other how to open the fridge door.

MAKING CONNECTIONS

Another form of learning is *associative learning*. You may have heard of Pavlov and his dogs, who started drooling whenever they heard a bell. In *classic conditioning*, a cat draws a connection between two stimuli. If the rustling of a bag of kibble is followed by some food in his dish, a cat will quickly see the link between these events and enthusiastically come running when he hears that particular sound.

A cat is quick to learn the sound of the refrigerator door and what it means

CONDITIONING

There is also a form of associative learning wherein the cat learns to connect her behavior to the consequences of that behavior. This is called *operant conditioning*. If your cat dislikes being brushed, and finds that you stop brushing her when she scratches your hand, she will do this increasingly often. Lashing out produces a desirable result for this cat: The scary brush disappears.

You might think, "What can I do with this?" but these learning principles are fairly essential, because as a cat owner you deal with them every day. When you want your cat to learn something, or learn *not* to do something, it helps to know exactly what's going on in that little head of his.

THE POWER OF REWARDS

Rewards, like punishment, play a central part in the "principles of learning"—the universal theory of learning new behavior, which applies to humans and animals, young and old alike.

REWARDING

By definition, rewarding your cat increases the desired behavior because it yields something fun or yummy for your cat. For example, you might reward your cat by giving him a treat when he walks into his cat carrier. (Trainers and behavioral experts prefer to talk about "reinforcement" rather than rewards, but I will use the latter term in this book.)

Receiving rewards is also important to us: Surely you would rather receive a compliment about your work from your coworker or supervisor than be scolded. And who doesn't reward themselves with something fun or delicious when they've finished a difficult task?

Rewards even work subconsciously: Social-media sites like Facebook and Instagram are addictive because getting a lot of likes on our latest post or photo activates our brain's reward system. Cats and kittens don't go on Facebook, but they are just as sensitive to rewards as we are.

How often do you reward your cat for something he has just learned or done well—for example, finally learning how to use the cat door? Probably less often than you could—but rewards are *so* important to a cat. A kitten has a lot to learn in his life, and that will go best if you consistently reward him when he does something well.

SUBCONSCIOUS OR UNINTENTIONAL REWARDS

As soon you say "reward," most everyone thinks you mean a treat or showing affection. Unless you are an animal trainer, you may well be unaware of many times that you've rewarded your cat.

One example is by feeding your cat when she meows early in the morning. You might have hoped to sleep longer, but in fact you have rewarded her behavior—so, the next day, she'll start meowing again (and maybe even earlier).

Rewards can also be indirect, without your involvement as an owner. For example, if your cat has ever found anything tasty on the counter, he will regularly look there to see if anything's been left behind to snack on. So long as you leave something on the counter now and again, even by accident, the cat gets his reward.

A piece of kibble or a treat is an immediate reward

THE RIGHT REWARD

Suppose you want to reward your cat intentionally. What should you use?

Some cats are crazy for food and will do anything for a treat or piece of kibble. These cats are easy to train. Just don't forget that treats and kibble mean extra calories: If you want to intensively train your cat or kitten, reduce their regular food portion a bit. Or make the rewards smaller—a small piece of a chew stick or a nibble of dried fish are just as good as bigger rewards.

Once you find something your cat will make an effort to get, it's best to save it for those times when you're training your cat.

Cats who are not motivated by food may be happy with some petting or playing. The latter can work well if you need your cat to get used to being brushed or combed, for instance.

Effective rewards

- Rewarding your cat always works better than punishment.
- Choose the reward that fits your cat: food, petting, or playing.
- Alternate rewards regularly, to keep your cat's attention longer.
- Give a reward immediately when your cat exhibits the desired behavior.

TO PUNISH OR NOT TO PUNISH?

Punishment is used much more often than rewards when dealing with cats. As soon as a cat does something wrong, many owners will spritz them with a spray bottle, startle them with a loud noise, or even give them a little slap. Unfortunately, I see a lot of unrecognized anxiety and stress in households where cats are punished unnecessarily. Punishment can cause considerable harm to a cat's well-being, so I'll delve fairly deeply into this topic.

PUNISHMENT

By punishing a cat, we hope that the undesirable behavior lessens or even stops. (Professionals usually use the word "correction" instead of "punishment"; I will use both terms interchangeably.)

Our usual idea of punishing a cat is to follow the undesirable behavior with something the cat doesn't like (the spray bottle, scare, or slap).

In a few specific situations, you can correct unwanted behavior by taking away something your cat likes. For example, if a kitten bites you while playing, stop playing: She will quickly make the association that biting = playing stops and will ultimately stop biting.

LEARNING YOUR LESSON?

Many people assume that punishment is the best way to teach a cat not to do something. We quickly turn to punishment when a cat does something wrong, even though we ourselves would really rather not be punished. (At work, you wouldn't learn a new task more quickly, or understand it better, if your boss punished you. Surely you'd instead hope for some understanding, patience, and extra clarification. It works exactly the same way with your cat!) What's more, forcing something on a cat always backfires, as she is accustomed by nature to make her own choices.

A FEELING OF POWERLESSNESS

When an owner wonders whether a cat can truly learn, they usually mean "Can I teach my cat *not* to do something?" and with the assumption, "In any case, I won't be able to succeed." So, punishments are mainly an expression of our own powerlessness or frustration. Why won't a cat stop scratching the couch or peeing next to the litterbox? In his eyes, a cat always has a good reason to behave a certain way. It is up to us, as cat owners, to figure out that reason. Only then can we do something about the behavior!

Punishment very often leads to fear

MISCONCEPTIONS

There are many misconceptions about punishment:

- "Mother cats punish their kittens, don't they?" Naturally, a mother cat will react if her kittens are really persistent in asking for attention—for example, by swatting or even walking away. But punishment in the sense of training ("You are not allowed to climb up onto the counter.") is not something a mother cat does.

- "You have to grab cats by the scruff of the neck, since that's what a mother cat does." A mother cat only picks up her kittens to move them when she thinks they are in danger or the nest is no longer safe. Incidentally, she never picks them up by the skin on the back of the neck—unless there is an emergency situation, in which case she may even grab them by the leg. Rather, she picks a kitten up by his whole neck, and she only does this while he is small enough to be carried.

- "If she goes outside the litterbox, you must rub a cat's nose in her pee." Unfortunately, this still happens much too often. It's a terrible punishment because cats are clean animals and can become panicked if their nose is pushed into pee or poop. And it doesn't serve any purpose, because a cat doesn't understand it.

- "I'm not punishing my cat; I'm just scaring her." This is a negative experience for a cat, so it is a form of punishment. What's more,

other cats in the house can also be frightened, although they haven't the foggiest idea what's going on.

WHY PUNISHMENT BACKFIRES

There are two reasons why punishment does not work:

- First, a cat simply doesn't understand it. If her litterbox seems gross to her, won't she simply find a clean place elsewhere? If her owner then rubs her nose in her pee, she'll find that traumatic but won't understand why they're doing it.

- Second, a cat doesn't learn what she *should* do through punishment. Rubbing her nose in her pee won't help her suddenly understand that she's expected to go in the dirty litterbox, instead of on the clean doormat.

WATCH OUT WITH PUNISHMENT

Punishment mainly has drawbacks. Sometimes an owner will cross a line without actually meaning to: They don't realize how much anxiety or stress they are causing for their cat.

- A cat never actually understands what she did wrong, so punishment just makes her life unpredictable and will ultimately lead to stress.

- A punishment may be so intense from the cat's perspective that he becomes permanently anxious.

- Never punish cats who are already frightened, or who pee outside their litterbox.

- Never punish a cat for natural behavior like scratching furniture, climbing, playing, or hunting. The most you can do is *redirect* this behavior to something you find acceptable, like using the scratching post.

- Never punish a cat physically; don't slap him or hiss in his face, as he may react aggressively. Also, picking up a cat to punish him may lead to his not wanting to be picked up anymore.

- Consider the intensity: Don't punish harder or more often if it isn't working. This is a common mistake. As a rule of thumb, if a cat does not change her behavior after her third "punishment," her owner has chosen the wrong approach and should try something else.

- Never have your cat come to you and then punish her. This is the best and quickest way to lose your cat's trust!

Why won't my cat stop misbehaving?

If your cat does not respond (satisfactorily) to your approach, this means his motivation to carry out the problem behavior outweighs the negative experience of his "punishment." The solution is not to punish even more, but to better examine your cat's motivations. His natural behaviors—like scratching—will continue even while he's *also* afraid of your reaction, because the urge remains so strong. So, the only result of punishment is lots of stress for your cat, plus a good chance that he'll misbehave again the minute you aren't there.

TAKING REVENGE?

There are owners who think their cat is consciously taking revenge or doing something to bug them, but this is nonsense: A cat chooses to do whatever benefits her. What you think as the owner is fairly insignificant to your cat!

Unfortunately, it's the relatively assertive cats who are punished most often, because owners think they have to show these cats who's boss. This outlook is totally backward: Assertive cats need *more* patience as they learn new behaviors. (They also have the highest chance of reacting aggressively to punishment.)

WHY A SPRAY BOTTLE DOESN'T WORK

All the drawbacks of punishment apply just as much to the oft-recommended spray bottle. Some cats aren't at all threatened by it, but I regularly see others who are afraid of anything that so much as sounds like a spray bottle—such as the hiss when you open a can of soda or beer.

You might suppose that a spray bottle does in fact work with your cat, because she jumps off the table when you make a move to pick it up. Not so! The fact that you keep having to grab the spray bottle every time means that your cat keeps exhibiting the unwanted behavior.

The only thing he learns from the spray bottle is that he must escape in time. Moreover, he is smart enough to continue carrying out the behavior in your absence.

TEACHING BOUNDARIES

Although we must be very careful with punishment, a cat still has to learn boundaries, of course. Every household has rules, and some of them will apply to your cat. When setting rules, consider what your audience can understand. Just as we talk differently to a two-year-old toddler and a 12-year-old rebel, we need to take a different approach to a kitten or cat than to a person. Your cat *cannot* think like a person—so, it's best if you can teach him not to do something without punishing him.

Punishment

- A cat won't actually learn what she should and shouldn't do through punishment!
- Punishment will change your cat's behavior, but almost never in the way you want.
- Punishment should never become your habitual reaction.
- Never punish a frightened cat!
- There is no "universal" punishment that works in all situations.

MODIFYING BEHAVIOR (WITHOUT PUNISHMENT)

What, then, is the best thing to do if your cat does something bothersome and you want to train him not to? In many cases, it may be enough to say "no." There is nothing wrong with issuing a small correction: Cats appreciate clarity. However, your reaction must suit both the situation and your cat.

KEY PRINCIPLES FOR CHANGING BEHAVIOR

These are the basic steps for changing any behavior:

1. Look into the cause of the behavior and the cat's motivation.

2. Offer her an alternative to the undesirable behavior.

3. Only then confront the undesirable behavior.

LOOK INTO THE CAUSE OR THE MOTIVATION

Teaching a cat *not* to do something means first looking carefully at *why* she is doing it—What is her underlying motivation?—although, admittedly, this is not always easy. A cat might scratch the furniture because she doesn't have a (good) scratching post. He might pee outside the litterbox because it's not clean enough, or urinating is painful. You must tackle this problem before you continue.

OFFER AN ALTERNATIVE

It's very important to offer an alternative so your cat can change her behavior. Maybe her scratching post is much too little and always falling over, so she goes looking for something sturdier. Buy a better post (see page 89)! In the latter case, clean your cat's litterbox: He may well return to it without complaint.

Above: A favorite scratching place

Right: If a cat occasionally finds something tasty on the counter, he'll check it out regularly

THEN TACKLE THE UNWANTED BEHAVIOR

Only once your cat has an alternative can you tackle the undesirable behavior—for example, by making the couch unappealing to scratch (see page 92).

AN EXAMPLE: GET OFF THE COUNTER

STEP 1: MOTIVATION

The counter is a wonderful place for a cat: Maybe she once found something to eat there; she can lick a pan clean, or drink from the faucet. Sometimes the counter is an ideal place to lie in the sun or to watch the neighbor cat in his front yard. In all these cases, your cat is (unintentionally) rewarded for her behavior.

STEP 2: ALTERNATIVE

If your cat likes to sit on the counter for a good view of the yard or street, offer her a different place to sit on a platform or climbing post (see page 85). If your cat likes to drink from the faucet, consider getting a drinking fountain or changing the location of her water bowls (see page 120).

STEP 3: DISSUASION

If your cat has been jumping on the counter for a long time, there's a good chance that she'll still do so, now and again. You can prevent this by making the counter permanently unattractive:

- Use aromas that a cat dislikes—for example, lemon peel or squeezes of toothpaste in little containers. Distribute these along the edge of the counter so your cat always comes across them upon jumping up.

- Lay something down that's unpleasant on the paws, such as doormats made of stiff artificial grass (available at a garden center or DIY shop) or rubber anti-slip bathmats with the nubby side up (cats don't like the little nubs on these mats).

Making something permanently unappealing works best because this doesn't depend on whether or not you're there. This approach also prevents your cat from using the "bad" behavior to get your attention. This method applies not only to counters, but anywhere your cat is not supposed to sit.

IGNORING UNWANTED BEHAVIOR?

On the internet, you'll often hear that "ignoring it" is the best approach to undesirable behavior. Unfortunately, that is not true in most cases.

- Ignoring a behavior does nothing to address the cause. For example, if your cat is bored and therefore meows to wake you up, you'll need to do something about the boredom first. Only once you've given your cat enough challenge can you ignore the midnight meowing.

- Ignoring often leads to frustration, and thus to more of the undesirable behavior.

- Ignoring is also very difficult, and there are few who have a good command of the art. We might start full of courage, but after a half hour of nighttime meowing most of us are so stressed or afraid of angry neighbors that we'll get up anyway to feed the cat. This creates extra difficulty, because now we've trained her to just keep at it longer. There is an old Dutch saying: "Whiners are not born, they are made."

THE TIME-OUT

Time-outs are another tool you can use when facing unwanted behavior: In the right situation, they really work well.

One such situation is when a kitten scratches or bites while playing, or keeps "tackling" your hands or feet even though you say "no." If she persists, give her a time-out by putting her out of the room: Pick her up calmly (never by the scruff of her neck), don't look at or talk to her (she'll perceive this as "attention"), and just put her in the hallway for a few minutes. Here, too, keep in mind that your kitten is so hectic because she has a huge need to play. A time-out does not reduce boredom, so providing lots of play or another kitten for companionship are good solutions.

REMOVING A CAT FROM THE GROUP

When there is friction in a group of cats, separating one cat for a bit can be a good idea just because it allows all the cats to settle down. But this doesn't actually train the "offending" cat to behave differently; he still hasn't the slightest idea what went wrong. If he was overly enthusiastic in approaching another cat, his need to play and run doesn't disappear with a time-out—at most it is suppressed (temporarily)!

TEACHING NEW BEHAVIOR

The life of a housecat looks very different from that of her ancestors. In the wild, a cat is sufficiently prepared for life if she can recognize enemies and dangerous situations, can hunt, and knows how to act toward other cats. A housecat has to learn a lot more, starting as a small kitten.

WHAT DO WE ASK OF OUR CATS?

For starters, we find "hunting" undesirable unless toy mice are the target, and we don't like cats to mark objects by scratching. Indoors, we expect a cat to adapt his natural behavior to our wishes and preferences.

A housecat has to get along with people, dogs, or other animals, and adjust to noises in the house and scary "monsters" like vacuum cleaners. Your cat will regularly be picked up, combed or brushed, and so on, and occasionally be put in a cat carrier. By nature, a cat is unused to all these things and will therefore have to learn them. How wonderful for you and your cat if this can be done stress-free!

A HELPING HAND

In practice, we owners often fall very short. Kittens don't go to "kitten classes" the way puppies go to puppy schools. Because of the stubborn misconception that cats can't be trained, we just let kittens do their thing. And when our little fluffball starts climbing the curtains or attacking ankles, out comes the spray bottle or some other deterrent.

Even if you could find a "kitty kindergarten," I wouldn't recommend it, because placing kittens in a new environment for training just doesn't work. They still need a helping hand, though! *You* are the best person to teach your cat what you expect in a suitable and—most importantly—loving way. Every owner owes their cat this helping hand!

A GOOD START

Of course, the very best time to start is when your kitten is still small. A kitten is curious by nature, sees everything as a game, and hopefully has not yet had any negative experiences that would make him fearful. But even if your kitten has already experienced something upsetting, you can still teach him new behavior—for example, that the cat carrier is not so scary after all.

Even adult cats can learn new or different behavior; it just takes a bit more time and patience than with kittens. The stronger the negative experience, the longer it will take. For example, if you've held your cat tightly in the past when brushing her or giving her pills, you'll first have to regain her trust.

Important things you can teach your cat or kitten

- Getting into the cat carrier trouble-free
- Not being afraid of the vacuum cleaner
- Letting you look at her teeth
- Letting you comb or brush her, hold her paws, and clip her claws

STEP BY STEP

There is only one way to teach such things as combing, clipping claws, or being picked up: step by step. (It's really no different than when you yourself learn a new skill, whether that's speaking a new language or making pottery.)

- First, "chunk" the behavior into small parts. I give a specific example below, but you can apply this principle to any new behavior.
- Practice each step repeatedly with your cat until it goes well.
- Reward your cat when he shows mastery of each step.

Cats can be easily distracted, so it's best to practice things briefly, multiple times a day

WHEN TEACHING YOUR CAT, CONSIDER HER CAPABILITIES

- A kitten is easily distracted and not always able to understand what you expect of him.
- Fearful cats need more time, of course.
- Not every cat is equally capable or clever, so be understanding when one of your cats learns something more slowly than his brother, or another cat.
- Character also plays a role: Outgoing cats learn easily, while timid cats need more time and a safe environment.

EXAMPLE: TEACHING COMBING OR BRUSHING STEP BY STEP

- Comb or brush your cat carefully, giving just one or two strokes at first.
- Limit yourself to areas that feel safe for your cat, like her head and shoulders.
- If your cat remains calm, reward her with a bit of a treat.
- The next time, brush your cat for two or three strokes and reward her.
- Keep the steps small and reward your cat after every combing session, no matter how brief it is.

CATS WHO ARE VERY SCARED OF THE BRUSH

Do you have a cat who starts running as soon as he sees you coming with the comb? Keep the comb or brush somewhere visible until your cat ignores it. The next step is to put a treat or piece of kibble next to it now and then. Once your cat dares to eat the treat, the next step is to pick up the comb when he is nearby. Reward him if he doesn't show any fear. Once your cat no longer runs away upon seeing the comb, you can carefully start combing as described above.

PETTING, OR: KEEP YOUR HANDS TO YOURSELF SOMETIMES!

Studies have revealed that petting our pets is a good stress-reliever for people, but for cats, unwanted petting can cause stress. We humans are fairly quick to touch or hug each other, whereas cats sometimes prefer to keep their distance.

A CAT'S BOUNDARIES

One cat is easier to get close to than another. This can be due to genetics, but the cat's experiences with people also play a role. If a kitten has had little contact with people during the first weeks of her life, she will have to gradually get accustomed to being touched. Another cat might have had negative past experiences with human hands—for example, because he was physically punished. Each cat can have her own reason to want to keep a distance.

THAT'S JUST THE SPOT ...

If your cat closes his eyes, purrs, turns parts of his body toward you, or pushes against your hand, you can be certain that he enjoys how you're petting him—and where. Every cat can differ in terms of where he likes to be petted. However, there are a few general guidelines.

For virtually all cats, the head and shoulders are "safe" places where you can always touch your cat. (These are also the parts of the body most cats allow other cats to groom.) Some cats find it annoying to be firmly petted along the back, but these cats may like to be briskly rubbed on their sides, for example.

... BUT DON'T GO THERE!

As you get closer to the tail (or actually the spot where the back meets the tail), you'll get more idiosyncratic responses. Some cats like this a lot

Respect your cat's boundaries

and will stand on their toes or even do a somersault. Other cats apparently don't like it: They'll make strange noises, lick their lips, growl, or exhibit other behavior that shows they don't like it. There are some theories about this, including that this part of the back is also stimulated during mating, but we don't actually have the slightest idea why cats react this way.

For many cats, the belly is another no-go area. Although a cat may roll on her back and show her tummy, this is not an invitation to pet her!

"Rubbing a cat the wrong way" is another classic warning, and in fact a correct one. Most cats really don't like to have their coats ruffled.

WARNING SIGNALS

A cat who does not want to be petted or have other physical contact will always give a warning. She points her ears backward and swishes her tail. If you continue petting her anyway, there is a good chance she'll take a

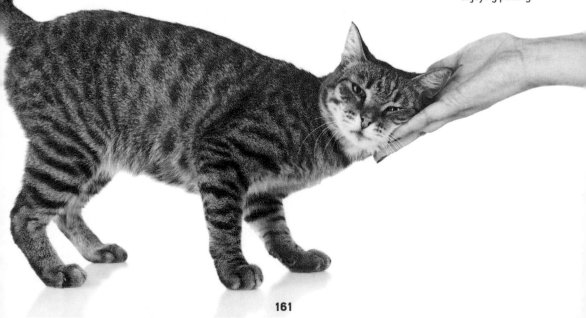

This cat is clearly enjoying petting

swipe with her claws. This is logical in her mind, because she already gave you a clear warning. Consistently overlooking her warnings increases the chance that a cat will skip them and lash out immediately.

Don't think that your cat has to learn to cooperate: Respecting your cat's boundaries is an essential component of your good relationship with her. (After all, we're not always in the mood to be touched, either!)

GETTING (RE)ACCUSTOMED TO PETTING

If your cat does not easily allow himself to be petted, you can get him used to it slowly. Pet him briefly (maybe even just once or twice) in a neutral, safe place, and stop before he gets restless. You can reward him occasionally with a treat after these sessions. Also, let your cat take the initiative: Research shows that when cats come to us on their own, they permit longer, more intense contact than when we make the first move.

Why does my cat lick herself after I pet her?

According to some, the cat's fur has been mussed, so he wants to smooth it back into place. But this question has never been studied, so there is no certain answer; it seems to depend greatly on the cat and the moment. You can pet a cat thoroughly one time, and another time, the lightest touch is enough to prompt a lengthy grooming session. Did he not want to be petted, or did your hand have an odd or unpleasant smell (to your cat)? Who can tell!

ILL OR IN PAIN?

If your cat suddenly does not want to be petted anymore or even reacts aggressively, there is a big chance she is ill or in pain. Consult your vet!

GREETING CATS

Are there rules about greeting a cat? And perhaps do we go a bit overboard in showering our cats with love? Either way, it's a good idea to stop and consider how we greet cats. Cats' behavior toward each other is considerably ritualized. If you don't know the rules, you can really flub up in a cat's eyes.

CATIQUETTE

There used to be books about etiquette explaining how we should act in certain situations. Now we think that's nonsense and prefer to act spontaneously and "naturally." But a cat actually thinks it's best if you follow "catiquette." My behavioral-therapy clients are always surprised when their cats come up to me during home visits; even cats who are usually afraid of visitors don't run away. The secret? Keeping my distance!

WHY DO CATS LIKE PEOPLE WHO DON'T LIKE CATS?

A cat likes to have control over his situation under all circumstances. He wants to wait and see what happens from a distance, and only then choose to walk up to someone, or not. He hates the pushy advances of people who come up to him talking and cooing, and immediately try to pet him. Many cats will experience this as overfamiliar.

It's not true that a cat will *always* sit with that person who doesn't like cats, but she does find it agreeable when a person ignores her at first. This is exactly what people who don't like cats do—so your cat is glad to finally meet someone who understands her!

THE RIGHT GREETING

Leave it to the cat to take the initiative by waiting until he comes to you. Calmly extend your finger or hand, but not in the exact direction of the cat. A hand stretched out toward his head or an approach from above can be a real threat to a timid cat. Let the cat come to you, and don't make your next move until he has finished sniffing you.

If he rubs his head against you: nice! You have been "approved" and now you can carefully pet him. But if the cat walks away, your chance at contact is gone for the moment. Maybe he will come out again later. Try not to pet him for now; that's very pushy—and definitely don't go after him; that would really be going too far!

PETTING, IN MODERATION!

When a cat has rubbed his head against you, that's usually a sign that it's fine for you to touch him. According to catiquette, you should limit yourself to his "safe" zones: the head and shoulders. If he accepts that as well, you can pet him elsewhere on his body. But be careful with the tummy!

Why does a cat turn his backside toward you?

Cats always greet each other in a set order: First they sniff nose to nose, then they rub against each other side to side, and then side to tail. They usually end by sniffing under each others' tails. So when your cat turns her backside toward you, she is giving you a chance to sniff . . . in her language, this is only polite!

First, give your cat a chance to rub her head against you

PICKING UP YOUR CAT

Does your cat love to be picked up and carried around in your arms like a baby? Or is she one of those cats who quickly puts up a fight? Quite a lot of cats don't really like being picked up or held.

RUNNING ON INSTINCT

By nature, a cat is an animal who flees from danger. When he doesn't trust something, he will first run away and then observe from a safe place to see whether there was actually cause for alarm. Accordingly, he always wants firm ground under his paws. Being picked up means losing control—and that's the last thing a cat wants.

RUNNING FROM THE PAST

Also, many cats have had negative experiences with being picked up, because when are the main times that we pick up a cat?

- When he's sitting somewhere that's not allowed (so, he's picked up and scolded at the same time).

- When it's time to put him in the cat carrier and go to the vet.

- When he's being punished (and possibly scruffed by the back of his neck).

- When he's being carried around (roughly) by small children—this definitely doesn't bear repeating!

GOOD INTENTIONS

Other negative experiences can arise from your good intentions, when you want to offer your cat safety or make something less scary for him. You might pick up your cat and carry him to meet visitors, or pick him up and put him near something he is not familiar with (a kitten, a new scratching post, etc.). This is really scary for your cat, because he'd rather decide for himself how and when he will check out a new object.

As much as you'd like to move your scratch-happy cat from your loveseat to her scratching post, you'll find she often runs away. Putting a cat somewhere against her will usually backfires!

The right way to pick up a cat

The best method is to put one hand under the cat's belly and to support his back paws with your other hand. If you want to hold him for a longer time, let him put his front paws on your arm or shoulder so he is sitting comfortably and relaxed. Don't hold him like a baby; most cats don't enjoy this!

Cats like to be held loosely, resting on your shoulder

Don't ever hold a cat by the scruff of the neck; this is really painful for an adult cat

TRAINING YOUR CAT TO BE PICKED UP

If a cat gets used to being carefully picked up from the time she is a kitten, she will allow this later without problems. For a (young) adult cat who doesn't like it, you can divide being picked up into small steps.

- Start by placing both hands against your cat's sides and applying slight pressure, for example, when he is on your lap. If he stays calm, reward him with a treat.

- Repeat this until he is used to it.

- Next, slide one hand under his belly and reward him if he stays calm.

- Next, exert a bit of upward force, without actually picking him up.

- The next step is to pick him up very slightly (about an inch) and then immediately put him back down, and so on.

ALTERNATIVES TO PICKING UP YOUR CAT

A cat needs her space. If the method described above doesn't seem to be working with your cat, let her be. My view is that a cat doesn't necessarily need to be picked up; it's only a worthwhile goal if she can truly get used to it.

If your cat doesn't want to be picked up but is not always easy to move when he is lying somewhere, use treats to teach him when he must jump down off something (for example, when he is sitting in your lap on the couch) or how to get into a cat carrier on his own (see page 157).

9

THE CAT CARRIER

Are vet visits something you (and your cat) would rather put off as long as possible because you don't look forward to putting your cat in her carrier? Or do you grit your teeth and forge ahead despite the scratches? In either case, this is a source of stress.

The good news is that you can get your cat used to the carrier, no matter her age or experience.

WHY GETTING USED TO THE CARRIER IS IMPORTANT

Postponing visits to the vet because of cat-carrier struggles is, of course, no good for your cat's health. And in an emergency, it can be of (life or death) importance that you get your cat into a carrier as quickly as possible. Also, a lot of hubbub catching your cat can mean that he arrives at the vet stressed out and unwilling to be treated.

A GOOD MEMORY

A cat can become panicked as soon as she sees her carrier, even if her last go-round was a year ago or more. With such cats, the common recommendation—to put the carrier in your living room a few days before your trip to the vet or kitty daycare—just isn't enough.

CHOOSING A CARRIER

Start by investing in a good cat carrier. A glued-together cardboard box will not work out to be more affordable in the long run. Just imagine if your cat escapes en route!

Here are some considerations when buying a cat carrier:

- The carrier has to be big enough that you can easily put your cat in and take him out. The best sort of carrier has a top you can remove completely; that way your cat can sit in the bottom half while on the vet's exam table, where his own scent will keep him calmer.

- If your cat is still young, buy a carrier with room to grow. A kitten will do just fine in a large carrier if you put some towels inside. But there's no putting a large cat in a small carrier!

- Opt for plastic: It's easier to clean if an "accident" happens along the way. You can also wash off those weird smells from visits to the vet.

- Make sure that the latches are secure and the door is sturdy enough. Your cat shouldn't be able to push through it in a blind panic.

- Wicker carriers may look cute, but they're a nightmare in reality. A cat sinks her claws into the weave, and is thereby impossible to get out of the carrier!

A STEP-BY-STEP PLAN

Always keep your carrier somewhere in your house that's easily accessible to your cat: in the living room or the cat room (if you have one). Put a pillow or blanket inside so the carrier is a nice place to sleep, and give your cat a treat or piece of kibble in the carrier every day. Once she expects these treats, start varying the time when you give them, so she is not surprised by the timing of her "carrier treat" on the day of a vet visit or other trip. Any change in routine raises big suspicions for a cat!

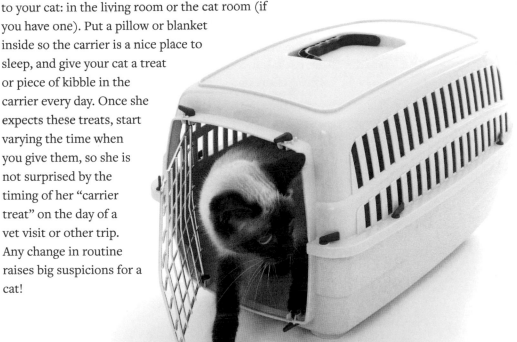

A carrier that opens from the front *and* the top is best

Frightened cats like having a towel draped over the cat carrier; they'll stay calmer in the dark

A SPECIAL PLAN FOR FRIGHTENED CATS

If your cat is scared to death of his carrier, use a different approach:

- Clean the carrier thoroughly with mild, unscented cleaner to remove any odors of sweat (i.e., fear) and the vet's office. If you doubt that your carrier is really suitable, buy a new one; you will have years of pleasure from it.

- Remove the top of the carrier, and leave the lower half in your living room or cat room with a blanket or pillow in it. Alternatively, put a towel over the carrier so it's less recognizable.

- Put a treat in the carrier every day, even if your cat doesn't yet dare to get it while you're there. This is important; it must really become a routine for your cat. If your cat is not motivated by tasty treats, you can tempt him by making his carrier part of playtime: Throw a ball or toy in the direction of the carrier. Once that goes well, throw the toy into the carrier itself. If he's very fearful, do this in small steps: Play very nonchalantly, closer and closer to the cat carrier.

- Next, teach him that he has to first step into the carrier before he gets a treat.

- Once your cat steps into the carrier with no problem, close the door for a second, and then open it immediately. Reward him with a treat if he stays calm. Practice this until the closed door does not stress him out anymore.

- Finally, you can pick up the carrier with your cat in it and walk around.

GETTING USED TO THE CAR

Your car poses additional stress factors: strange smells and noises (intense for a cat). Let your cat get accustomed slowly, by just putting the carrier in the car at first. The next time, go on to start the car. Finally, drive a short distance.

CARRIER DON'TS

- It's best not to force your cat into her carrier (unless an emergency situation occurs before she's finished training), as this will lay the foundation for permanent fear.

- Don't put two cats in one carrier, even if they're going to the vet at the same time and they easily fit. Such a time is too traumatic for them to be shut up together in a small space. If they become stressed, they will take it out on each other.

- Don't ambush your cat while she is sleeping to pop her into the carrier.

BUT WHAT IF THERE IS AN EMERGENCY?

Place the carrier with the door facing upward, and lower in your cat, rear paws first. This way (as opposed to head first), he can't brace himself with all four feet to resist. With cats who are very scared, it can work well to quickly throw a towel over your cat and then put her in the carrier, towel and all. In either case, a carrier that can open from the top is very helpful.

This cat is not impressed by this carrier

10

GOING TO THE VETERINARIAN

Once you've gotten your cat used to the carrier it's on to the next step: a visit to the vet!

HELLO, KITTY!

If your kitten has never been to the vet, she will naturally not have any negative feelings yet. Try to keep it this way! Many vets are glad to have you come by with your kitten for a trial run or during dedicated "kitten office hours." Often, they'll briefly examine your kitten (without giving any shots, as yet), and leave time for her to calmly walk around and receive a treat from you or the assistant. Such a relaxed visit is the perfect start.

CAT-FRIENDLY PRACTICES

There are many strategies to make vet visits less stressful for adult cats, as well. It starts with choosing the right vet. There are some vets who are very good at medicine, but less great at actually interacting with cats. If your cat is very frightened at the vet's, you might consider going to a different one.

These days, vets can be certified as Cat Friendly Practices by the American Association of Feline Practitioners. There are even special clinics that treat only cats. Certifications aside, the most important thing is that you and your cat like your chosen practice. (If your cat is still being pulled out of the carrier by the scruff of his neck, I personally would consider going to a different clinic.)

IN THE WAITING ROOM

A cat-friendly practice will have a separate waiting room for cats, or elevated places where you can set down your cat carrier. But if this is not the case, no problem: Put your cat carrier on the chair next to you, out of reach of other animals and children. Here, too, draping a towel over the carrier can be helpful. Never put your cat carrier on the ground: Dogs, and the feet of passers-by, will be too close—and therefore threatening—to your cat.

Try to arrive as close to your appointment time as possible, so your wait will be short. If the waiting room is full of other cats and dogs, ask the receptionist whether your cat can wait behind the counter.

IN THE EXAM ROOM

- Closely observe your cat's reactions in the exam room. It's best to examine some cats immediately (before they become panicked). Other cats need a little extra time to become acclimated, and are best left in their carrier for a bit before the vet's examination starts.

- Ask your vet to let your cat sit in (the bottom part of) her carrier as much as possible, so long as this does not disrupt her treatment.

- A very frightened cat may like it if you put a towel over her head, since what a cat doesn't see doesn't exist for her. Some cats will prefer to put their head under your arm or in your jacket; let them do it.

- Don't hold your cat too firmly: The tighter you hold him, the greater the chance he will fight back and wrench himself free. In most cases, it is enough to loosely wrap your arms around your cat, whereas grabbing a cat by the scruff of his neck will lead to a lot more stress—now, and at the next visit.

This vet is taking her time with this cat

HOME AGAIN

Wash your cat carrier thoroughly with a mild, unscented cleanser so that all the annoying odors are gone, then put it back in its familiar place and resume your routine of leaving a treat inside daily. Your cat might not be fooled immediately, but after a few days you'll be back on track.

FIGHTING AFTER A VISIT TO THE VET

Sometimes a catfight will break out when you bring one of your cats home from the vet. These fights can be particularly intense, but the good news is that you can prevent them.

WHO'S THAT NEW CAT?

A cat who has been to the vet smells different: She takes on the odor of disinfectants, medication, or her own fear (sweat). The cat who stayed home no longer recognizes his housemate, or responds to the smell of fear that surrounds her. Unusual movements (such as staggering after anesthesia) or a new cone around your cat's head can cause also great confusion for the cat who stayed home. If you're lucky, your other cats will wash the cat who came back from head to toe, getting rid of all those scary odors so that she smells familiar again. Unfortunately, sometimes the other cats immediately attack.

HOW TO STOP A FIGHT BEFORE IT STARTS

If your cats get to the point of hissing and growling, you must take action to prevent an actual fight:

- Immediately separate them: Put the cat who went to the vet in a separate room so all your cats can calm down. This can take anywhere from a few hours to two full days. It's better to err on the side of more time, since cats really don't forget each other in just a few hours.

- Before she rejoins the other cats, rub the cat who went to the vet with something that will smell familiar, such as the blanket she sleeps on or an item of your own clothing out of the laundry basket—anything so long as it has a homey smell.

- When your cats have calmed down, you can carefully open the door. Make sure they don't immediately run toward each other! If they have an intense reaction, close the door right away, then keep them separated for another day or longer, and finally do a reintroduction. You can use the step-by-step plan for introducing a new cat on page 68.

- If there is tension but not actual fighting, you can use a temporary gate or another barrier. That way, your cats can see each other but can't get too close to each other.

PREVENTING PROBLEMS

Naturally, it's better to prevent problems in the first place. Even if your cats are best friends, a visit to the vet can be a radical change, although it seems minor to us. It is best to make the following measures a standard ritual, especially if there has already been an altercation after a previous vet visit.

- After your cat sees the vet, always allow him to recover at home in a separate room until he is completely clearheaded and relaxed, however long this takes.

- Rub him down with his own scent or yours (as above).

- Be careful if your cat is wearing a cone or has a new cast. Keep your other cat(s) at a distance until they are used to their housemate's new "look."

Cats can be frightened if their housemate suddenly comes home wearing a cone. Fortunately, this cat is okay with it.

12

THE VACUUM CLEANER

Although there are cats who allow their coats to be vacuumed with no problem, most are (logically) quite afraid of the big, noisy monster. For a cat, who has much keener hearing and a far more sensitive nose than we do, the roar and the electrical smell are nearly intolerable. Fortunately, vacuum cleaners are becoming ever smaller and quieter, and there are even cute little robot vacuums.

GETTING USED TO THE VACUUM

Since you will be vacuuming regularly, it's helpful if your cat can overcome this fear (or at least be less afraid). There are several methods, but this is the easiest: The key idea is to let your cat slowly get used to the vacuum cleaner without having to get too close to the thing.

- When you want to vacuum, close the door to the room your cat is in, at the moment. Vacuum the whole house except that room, then tuck away your machine (it really has to be out of sight!) and open the door to that room again.

- Calmly let your cat do his thing, then, only once your cat is in another room, close *that* door and clean the room you skipped. Then, hide the vacuum away again. This way you'll make sure your cat can't see the vacuum cleaner and only hears the noise from a distance.

- After a few weeks (or months, depending on your cat's fear level), leave the door of the room your cat's in slightly open while you vacuum. Do this for a few weeks.

- Once your cat is no longer bothered, enter her room with the vacuum cleaner, but leave it off until your cat has decided for herself whether she wants to stay or go. Once she has decided, you can start vacuuming. Make sure your cat always has a clear path to leave the room, and never move directly toward her with the vacuum cleaner.

PART 5

Playing and training

WHY PLAY IS IMPORTANT

We still don't know exactly why animals play. Some ethologists (who study animal behavior) think that animals can't play, and what appears to be fun and games is actually instinctive. These are usually the same scientists who say animals don't have any emotions. Others theorize that play mainly helps animals learn: By jumping and wrestling, kittens practice for the real hunt.

THE BENEFITS OF PLAY

Nowadays, the idea of play as practice is a bit outdated. Of course, a kitten's movements will get faster and more precise the more he plays, but this isn't the only reason kittens frolic around. The neuroscientist Jaak Panksepp says playing teaches social rules: In other words, when kittens play, they're learning how to get along with others (Panksepp, 2007).

Another very important—and surprising—effect of play takes place in the brain: Five minutes of play per day can reverse the effects of long-term stress. When cats play, their brains produce certain neurotransmitters that combat stress more effectively than any sedative.

EVEN MORE REASONS TO PLAY

If you still aren't completely convinced that play is important for your cat, here are three more reasons every cat needs to play:

- Play is healthy: Lots of movement keeps a cat fit, prevents obesity, and ensures she stays in good condition as she ages—the same benefits that people get from regular exercise!

- Play prevents boredom: There's still a hunter underneath your cat's silky fur, and using her natural instincts is essential to a happy, fulfilled life.

- Play is fun! Someone once told me that her cat "glows" when he plays. I can really relate to this; cats truly put their heart and soul into their play.

BOREDOM = MISCHIEF

The Dutch word for "mischief" is *kattenkwaad*, which translates literally to "cat wickedness." There's good reason for this expression: Cats are very talented when it comes to mischief, as you can see from countless videos on the internet.

STIMULI ALL AROUND, OR NOWHERE TO BE FOUND?

Boredom—that is, a lack of stimuli and opportunities to let off steam—is the underlying cause of feline mischief. When a cat hunts, all of his senses are on high alert; searching for prey involves lots of new stimuli. Since the last time he hunted, all kinds of things have happened in his territory: Rain changed the odors, a dog went by, another cat sprayed, or a big branch fell down across his regular path. All of these changes must be sniffed and evaluated.

It's not difficult to imagine how much sensory input a cat experiences as she walks outside, especially compared to an indoor cat's less complex life. No matter how tall and exciting your cat's scratching post is, it stays in the same place day in and day out, and it will never smell any different. The same goes for all the balls and toy mice gathering dust under your couch. After a few days, the novelty wears off and they become as (un)interesting as the furniture they're underneath.

THE DANGERS OF BOREDOM

Indoor cats can certainly become bored despite your best intentions. Some cats will sleep more if they don't have anything to do, while others will shred your curtains or take out their extra energy on another cat. This is logical: If there's nothing happening in the house, wouldn't you want to *make* something happen? Cats' reactions to boredom can be harmful; for example, a cat who becomes stressed out may lick himself bald or obsessively chase his tail (see page 36).

GIVE ME ATTENTION!

Cats come up with their own entertainment, and your cat will quickly realize that making you part of the game is extra fun. Scratching the wallpaper or creeping along the bottom of the couch is already a nice game, but it's even more exciting for your cat if you immediately respond to his antics. Attention—even negative attention—is a reward.

Knocking things over is a fun game!

If your cat is causing mischief, observe him closely to figure out whether his behavior is a call for attention, or if something else is going on. A cat who wants to scratch the couch walks right up to it and sinks his claws into the fabric. A cat who wants attention starts with a bit of pacing. If that doesn't catch your eye, he'll walk theatrically toward the couch while keeping one eye on you. (And if you don't react to that, your cat will probably still proceed to scratch your couch!)

In the case of boredom or attention-seeking, punishment is obviously not the right idea: It solves nothing because your cat will just become more frustrated (see page 148). Plus, punishment doesn't do anything to meet his need for play and challenges. Next I'll discuss engaging your cat with toys and games instead!

Why does my cat knock things off the table?

A cat's paws are engineered to catch and hold prey—and they're also helpful tools for investigating unknown objects. By tapping something carefully, a cat learns all kinds of things: Is it alive? Is it dangerous? Is it heavy?

An object falling off the table (accidentally) stimulates your cat's hunting behavior, rewarding him and giving him reason to do the same thing again. Sending your possessions crashing to the ground can also be attention-seeking behavior: If you react to objects being knocked over, your cat quickly learns this is an excellent way to get your attention.

Why does my cat run around the house like crazy?

Most cats—whether they're indoor or outdoor, old or young—occasionally get the "zoomies." When this happens, kittens and cats alike "go crazy" running through the house or chasing each other. There's no research on this behavior, but it often happens in the evening or around dusk, so it likely has something to do with hunting. Maybe it's a warm-up for the real thing? In any case, don't join in on the fun; sometimes your cat wants to go crazy on his own!

For a kitten, the whole world is a playground

YOUR CAT'S TOYBOX

We all want to make our cats happy—and manufacturers take advantage by filling pet-store shelves with all kinds of toys, to say nothing of the ever-more-numerous websites selling special cat toys. It's quite tempting to stock up, because more toys mean more fun, right?

THE PURRFECT TOY

Toy preferences differ from cat to cat: Some are crazy about mice or balls, while others prefer to chase strings or leap after wand toys.

Kittens will play with a stuffed toy mouse as if it is another kitten, whereas adult cats view toys as prey. If it's the size of a prey animal and has fur or feathers, your cat is sure to like it. If it moves, even better! According to a study by John Bradshaw, cats find it especially exciting when a toy breaks (Bradshaw, 2013). This doesn't mean your cat revels in destruction. Rather, when something breaks, it changes—and anything new or different is interesting to your cat.

FORGOTTEN UNDER THE COUCH?

No matter how much your cat loves her toys, she will get sick of them at some point. It's important to alternate toys regularly to give her new stimuli.

To keep your cat's playthings feeling fresh and fun, start by getting all of her toys out from under the couch and putting them in a closed box. Take two or three out every day, and put yesterday's choices back in the box.

But what if your cat just doesn't like a particular toy anymore? Buying something similar made from a different fabric or with a different smell will catch her interest again!

Don't leave your cat alone with string; swallowing it can cause intestinal problems

DIY CAT TOYS

When it comes to creating your own toys, keep it simple. A cardboard box or a paper bag (without handles to get tangled in!) is already a party for many cats. Every DIY toy is something different that offers a new challenge.

Balls of wadded-up paper are usually quite entertaining for your cat, and even ripping a piece of paper can be enough to get her attention. See how your cat watches excitedly while you crinkle the wad of paper, waiting until the ball is ready for play.

ENGAGING THE SENSES

Good toys stimulate multiple senses: hearing, smell, touch, and sight. Bird feathers are appealing because of their smell, while a box of autumn leaves is exciting because of its smell and rustling sound.

Some cats love to play with water; for them, a big tub of water plus some mechanical swimming fish or pieces of kibble to "catch" is a wonderful new experience. You can set this up in the bathroom now and then, or out on the balcony or patio in the summer.

SMELLS AS ENRICHMENT

You can buy many toys with added catnip or valerian. Not all cats respond to these herbs; it's estimated that one in three cats lacks the gene (or genes—the precise mechanism is still unknown) to detect these scents. Cats who are crazy about valerian don't necessarily respond to catnip, and vice versa.

CATNIP

Catnip has as a special effect on cats. When your cat is "high" on catnip, you might notice her sniffing around intensely; rubbing her head, cheeks, or chin on her catnip-scented toy; or drooling. These behaviors aren't sexual in origin, by the way; they seem to be serendipitous: The allomone (chemical) that happens to attract cats to catnip plants is actually produced to repel leaf-eating insects (Bol, 2017). Catnip doesn't affect very young cats; kittens don't react to it until they're at least three months old.

VALERIAN

Valerian is an herb with a similar effect to catnip. It's less often used in toys, but if you do some searching, you can find pillows filled with valerian at pet stores. (You'll have the best luck shopping online.)

Don't leave toys with catnip or valerian lying around: Cats get used to the smell quickly, causing it to lose its effect.

MATATABI

Matatabi is another smell that cats find delightful. You won't find it in toys, but rather in the form of chewing sticks. Matatabi is the dried stem of a kiwi-like plant called silver vine (*Actinidia polygama*).

ROBOTIC TOYS

You can also buy toys that move independently, whether they "wind up" or run on batteries. There are mechanical mice, "undercover mice" that run in circles beneath a mat, and interactive, spinning teaser toys that make a furry or feathery "critter" bob like a butterfly at the end of a wand. If your cat has a lot of energy, these toys can keep her occupied while you're away.

Be alert about the quality of these products, especially if you buy them online from another country. Toys should be safe for your cat and shouldn't break, have loose pieces, risk entangling her—or cause frustration because she can't quite catch them.

LASER TOYS?

Lasers are very popular with cats, but they're also (rightly) the subject of debate. A laser's light can damage your cat's eyes, which is why some veterinarians strongly advise against them. Here's how to make laser play safer and more fun for your cat:

- Make sure not to shine a laser in your cat's eyes. A "laser bolt" (a laser light on a stand that revolves by itself) is unsafe because you can't control where it points.

- Never allow small children to play with a laser; they can't aim well and could accidentally shine it in your cat's face.

- Cats can become frustrated with lasers. When a cat hunts, he's supposed to catch prey, so it's annoying if he fails to capture anything over and over again. End the game by focusing the light on a piece of food, a treat, or a ball so your cat can "catch" something and end up satisfied.

- If your cat keeps looking for the light even after you've stopped playing, then a laser isn't a suitable toy for him.

APPS FOR CATS?

Today, you can find apps for your tablet or cell phone specifically designed for your cat to play. These games have the same downfall as lasers: Your cat can't get the satisfaction of catching a mouse on a screen. It's OK to let your cat play these virtual games in moderation, but make sure to play with more traditional toys, too.

Left- or right-pawed?

While your cat is playing, check to see whether he has a preferred paw when tapping balls or toy mice. One study revealed that female cats use their right paw more often, while male cats tend to be left-pawed (Wells and Millsopp, 2009)!

A cardboard box guarantees endless fun

PLAY IS MORE THAN HAVING TOYS

Of course play is important. But isn't it enough for your cat to have a mountain of mice and balls to choose from? And what if you don't have much time to play?

NEVER STOP PLAYING

Having a lot of toys is never a substitute for physical activity. It's important for owners to add extra challenges to their cats' lives. We all play with our kittens, partly because kittens are so playful—but don't forget your adult cat!

Even if you have multiple cats, it's important to take time for play every day. Play is good for your bond with your cat, and even stimulates her to romp around and exercise more on her own.

Similarly, even if your cat goes outdoors, it's still a good idea to play with her. Going outside doesn't necessarily mean she's getting tired out: Some cats stroll through the yard, take a nap under a bush, and come back feeling rested.

PUZZLE FEEDERS

Puzzle feeders are all the rage right now. These are toys that hold kibble or treats and make your cat put in effort to get them out, such as a ball that dispenses one piece of food each time your cat taps it. A homemade puzzle feeder could be a pyramid built from toilet-paper rolls. Puzzle feeders are becoming better and more creative, and you can find one to suit just about any cat. (Have a look at foodpuzzlesforcats.com!)

BENEFITS

Puzzle feeders offer benefits even beyond fun and stimulation. If your cat gobbles his food too quickly, adding a mental challenge to mealtime will slow him down.

A puzzle feeder is a nice addition, but not a replacement for playing!

An overweight cat will also benefit from a puzzle feeder: Because she can only eat a small amount at a time, she'll feel full sooner and potentially lose weight.

DRAWBACKS

Unfortunately, some cats don't understand puzzle feeders at all. If your cat still doesn't get it with some help and direction, you should stop using this toy. A puzzle should be a source of enrichment for your cat, not frustration! You can always come up with alternatives that fit your cat better. For example, you could toss pieces of kibble across the room for him to "catch" one by one.

Puzzle feeders stimulate your cat's hunting behavior but don't necessarily involve a lot of exercise. They can be valuable challenges for your indoor cat, but they're not replacements for play that involves running and jumping!

ON THE MOVE

Physical exercise is very important for cats, so make sure to encourage your cat to run, jump, and climb her cat tree. Strings or wand toys are especially useful for getting your cat moving. Throwing balls or mice also works well, although cats can quickly become bored with these kinds of toys. Engaging your cat with toys on sticks can trigger her to play longer and more intensely than batting around a ball by herself, because movement stimulates her hunting instinct.

Play more carefully with senior cats, as jumping and quick turns can be painful for them.

TEACHING YOUR CAT TO PLAY (AGAIN)

Nothing is as frustrating as a cat who yawns and looks away while you're giving it your all with the expensive new wand toy. Maybe you've never played with your cat before, and now she has to get used to your sudden desire to play. Maybe you quickly put the wand away if your cat doesn't enthusiastically chase it after a few seconds of swishing it around. By the time she thinks it might be fun to participate after all, you're already scrolling on your phone. Your cat needs time to get accustomed to the idea of playing—and maybe get used to an unfamiliar toy, too:

- Plan a set time for play, preferably when your cat is a bit livelier. For most cats, that's in the evening.

- Choose a toy that your cat thinks is extra fun, or try out an exciting new toy.

- Be patient: Even if your cat doesn't immediately join in, don't be disappointed. Your cat doesn't mean it personally! Consistently offer your cat a string, wand toy, or ball at the same time every evening, and watch carefully for the first sign of interest.

- Keep at it: Your cat may join in hesitantly at first, but after a few days, he'll be waiting eagerly for playtime. Then, you can build up to longer play sessions.

- A few minutes of play is already quite a bit to start with, especially if your cat is older. Be happy for every step you take together.

How long should I play with my cat?

The length of your cat's playtime depends on many factors, including her age. Kittens and very young cats are almost insatiable: They can play for a half hour or longer and still not get tired out. Energetic cats can play for a long time even when they're older, while others give up after five or ten minutes. That's not a bad thing—it just means your cat can't focus her attention on one thing for longer than that. It's best to play for five minutes a few times a day if that's as long as your cat wants.

THIS CAT WILL PLAY, AND THAT CAT WON'T!

Sometimes cats in the same household have totally different play requirements—for example, if you have a young, assertive kitten and an older cat. The kitten always wants to play; the older cat doesn't (anymore). In this case, you should play with your kitten more so he burns off that extra energy. The same goes for mismatched adult cats: Play more with the active cat so the other can get some rest.

I'm a big proponent of taking action to prevent tension. If you think one cat is bothering the other, distract him! It's often easy to tell that a cat is bored and looking for excitement—for example, if you see him creeping up on his sleeping sister. Throw a toy to the mischief-maker in time to draw his attention away.

A simple string is already plenty of fun for most cats

MAKING PLAY FUN

How to play with your cat isn't always obvious. As much as we try, many owners aren't very good at it, or have a different idea of "playing" than our cats do.

ON THE HUNT

Imitating prey is the best way to make play fun for your cat. Try to imagine how a mouse would behave, and move the toy accordingly. A mouse might sit still for a moment, then suddenly scurry away to disappear. A moment later, it'll appear again and run farther away. Give your cat the chance to behave like the hunter she is: She'll notice the prey, lie in wait, wiggle her hindquarters, and then leap at her prey the moment it's still.

IN THE RIGHT DIRECTION

Prey never runs *toward* a cat, so always throw mice, balls, and other objects in the opposite direction from your cat. He'll be more excited by something that's moving away from him rather than toward him.

AT A DISTANCE

Your cat can't see objects clearly within about one foot of her face, so don't dangle wand toys or strings too close to her head. She also doesn't like having things pushed against her snout: She may still swat the toy away, but this is more likely out of irritation than playfulness.

ON THE GROUND

Your cat's most common prey is mice, so he'll mainly react to movements on the ground. Some cats don't even understand that toys can fly through the air, or will give up on them more quickly than a toy that's pulled along the ground.

OUT OF SIGHT

A mouse that's being chased will hide in a hole, or burrow under a layer of leaves. You can achieve this effect yourself by making a string or wand toy disappear under an old towel, behind a cushion, or around a corner. Success is guaranteed, especially if you move the "prey" slowly or in short spurts.

CHANGING SPEED

Swishing a wand toy back and forth quickly might seem like a good approach, but this can be frustrating for your cat because he can't keep up. Instead, vary the tempo: Make your cat run for a moment, then switch speeds and move the string tantalizingly slowly.

MAKING THE CATCH

The aim of hunting is to catch prey, so give your cat regular chances to catch her toy or ball; otherwise, she might become bored after just a little while.

IS PLAYTIME OVER?

Don't stop playing if your cat is just getting going: This will leave him either frustrated or looking for another way to expend some energy. He might go bother his brother, or start hunting your feet or hands to keep the game going. It's especially important to keep hyperactive cats and young kittens from doing this (more below).

Some cats suddenly plop down on the ground, seeming to lose interest in play. This may be a fake-out; you can usually reengage these cats after a few minutes' rest.

LOOK MA, NO HANDS!

Never let your cat play with your hands, and don't encourage this behavior with your kitten.

It's all too easy to accidentally incite "rough" play or wrestling by rubbing your cat's belly: He will almost always react instinctively by grabbing your hand or arm with his forepaws and kicking with his back legs. This seems funny when a kitten is small, but once he's grown, he can scratch or bite you quite hard—and by then it's much more difficult to train him not to do this.

Wiggling your fingers under your blanket or along the edge of the table is a variation on this theme: This teaches your cat that your fingers are a toy. You shouldn't be surprised if he exhibits finger-hunting behavior at other, more unwanted times—for example, when you're turning a page in your book. Your cat won't understand why he can play with your fingers at one time but gets punished for doing it another time.

My cat plays fetch! Is he a genius?

Many more cats play fetch than you might think! Playing fetch is a learned behavior: Your kitten (or cat) runs around with a toy and accidentally lets it drop near you. You pick it up and enthusiastically throw it. That's fun for your cat because he gets to keep playing, so he is rewarded for "fetching" his toy and may well exhibit this behavior again. But you can still tell your friends he is a genius!

PLAYING ALONE

Not all forms of play are social: Cats do like to play alone now and then—say, by running after a ball or ripping up a wad of paper. At these times, your cat usually won't like it if you join in. Let your cat do her thing; there will be plenty of other opportunities for you to join the fun!

HYPERACTIVE CATS?

Can a cat play *too* much? There are certainly cats who never seem to get enough. Both their character and environment can bring this about; one cat simply needs more excitement, by nature, than the next. Kittens are inexhaustible, which is one reason I recommend adopting two kittens at once, and even adult cats can remain very active to the point of being bothersome.

OVERSTIMULATION

As odd as it sounds, some cats have an insatiable appetite for play because they get *too much* stimulation. Cats who are enticed to play again and again but never get to really finish a game can remain hyperalert even after playtime ends. A cat like this benefits from clearly structured playtimes: Hold play sessions long enough to tire him out, and let him rest at other times.

There are also those cats with a particularly great need for challenge. If that's your cat, you can take playtime to the next level by training your cat!

TRAINING YOUR CAT

If your cat is very adventurous, or you'd like to do more than just play with her, you really can train your cat! Just as some dogs do agility training, certain cats enjoy running an obstacle course or learning to do other things.

MORE THAN JUST TRICKS

The idea of training a cat has negative connotations for many people. "Why would you train a cat to do tricks?" they might ask, implying that training is demeaning to animals or ill-suited to cats. Of course, that's not the idea at all: Training isn't something you do *to* your cat, but rather *with* your cat—because it's fun for both of you. After all, it would be impossible to train a cat to do anything unless she enjoyed it!

Cats with oodles of energy (like Bengals, Sphynxes, and Eastern breeds) may especially enjoy training.

STARTING SIMPLE

In essence, training your cat is simply rewarding desirable behavior. If you've used treats to teach your cat to get into his carrier, for example, you've already made a good start (see page 146).

A simple trick to get your cat started with training is teaching him to follow your finger: Begin by holding a treat and having your cat walk a few steps toward it; only then let him eat it. You can build on this until he follows the treat reliably.

THE NEXT PHASE

Once your cat follows a treat like a pro, teach him to follow your finger or empty hand instead. Reward him with a treat only after he follows your finger for a few steps in the right direction. Gradually extend this skill by having him walk alongside you or "weave" between your legs.

Once your cat has the hang of this, you can teach him to jump down from the couch by following your hand or finger (instead of constantly having to move him yourself)! Or you can teach him to jump on or over something else, like a chair. Once he's doing that, you're already on the way to a full agility course! Of course, a treat must follow every step of progress.

CLICKER TRAINING

Dogs are often trained with a "clicker," a small device that makes a clicking sound when you press it. You can use a clicker, too; it works as something of a "bridge" to the behavior you want to teach.

First, teach your cat that the clicker sound means he'll get a treat. Once he understands that, hearing the click becomes a reward in itself, since it's followed by something tasty. A clicker is helpful because you can use it to reward your cat at the *exact* time he behaves in the desired way (without wasting time fishing a treat out of your pocket).

Although you *can* use a clicker to train cats, it's not necessary: You can train your cat just fine with treats alone. If you do want to try clicker training, start by taking a class to learn the basics and avoid approaching it incorrectly. You can also find helpful books such as Karen Pryor's *Clicker Training for Cats*, as well as lots of information on the internet.

CAN EVERY CAT BE TRAINED?

The hardest part of training your cat is finding the right reward. If your cat is crazy about treats or kibble, you're already in a good position. Unfortunately, some cats aren't motivated by food, but you can pet or cuddle them as a reward instead. If your cat isn't interested in either, then it will be rather difficult to train her.

Training is easiest if you start right away when your cat is a young kitten, but you can also train adult cats with a bit of patience. The more adventurous your cat, the more likely she'll participate.

Clicker training

TURNING AN OUTDOOR CAT INTO AN INDOOR CAT

There are all kinds of reasons why your outdoor cat might have to become an indoor cat. The change could be temporary; for example, your cat may need to stay inside for a few weeks after a move, or circumstances like a noisy holiday or a big snowstorm could make the outdoors temporarily unsafe for him. Your cat might also have to stay indoors permanently if you move from a house with a yard to an apartment.

MAKING THE INDOORS EXCITING

Whatever the reason for the change, pay extra attention to your cat's well-being.

Everything I've already described in this book is even more important if your outdoor cat needs to stay inside: Keeping toys varied, playing in the right way, and making sure that play is really fun for your cat are all key. Above all, try to stimulate "hunting" behavior at playtime (see page 192).

ESTABLISHING A ROUTINE

Make sure to play with your cat at two set times (at least) each day, with one session in the evening (around the time your cat is usually active). This is important for two reasons: First, cats love routine in general, and second, a fixed schedule makes it easier for your cat to get used to indoor play. The more positive challenges she has, the easier your cat's transition will be.

BRINGING THE OUTSIDE IN

Bringing enrichment from outside into your home is extra-interesting for your former outdoor cat: think autumn leaves, bird feathers, or sticks. These days, you can even buy a sort of grass mat (made from real lawn grass growing in a box) for that authentic outdoor feeling.

PART 6

A healthy cat is a happy cat

HOW CAN I TELL IF MY CAT IS IN PAIN?

We'd rather not think about it, but a cat will likely experience pain at some point in his life. It's important to recognize pain at the first sign, because cats hardly ever let it show: It's dangerous for a solitary animal to show weakness, since enemies are always watching, ready to pounce. An injured cat can lose her territory to a rival, or be attacked by a weaker cat who usually wouldn't dare.

HIDING PAIN

Many owners have gone to the vet with a cat who was limping or otherwise showing pain at home, only to watch her walk around the exam room with no problem. So it's always a good idea to take a video of your cat's behavior at home to help the vet make a diagnosis.

Problems lurking inside a cat's mouth are notoriously hard to catch at the onset. By the time a cat stops eating, his mouth or teeth are often already very infected; he may even have tumors of the mouth. It's almost unimaginable how much pain cats can tolerate. Checking your cat's mouth on a regular basis yourself and seeing the vet yearly are key preventative steps.

Bladder problems are also overlooked far too often in cats because some owners have misconceptions about how they cause a cat to behave (see pages 135 and 204).

MEOWING IN PAIN?

It's rare for a cat to meow in pain—although it's more likely in certain situations, as with urinary infections. You can't say that a cat isn't in pain because he *isn't* meowing: Too often, cats will suffer in silence.

How well do you know your cat?

As an owner, you should observe your cat closely and know what his normal behavior looks like. How often does he pee and poop in ordinary circumstances? How much does he sleep? What are his normal eating and drinking routines? Sudden behavior changes can indicate pain or illness and should be checked out by a vet.

HOW A CAT SHOWS PAIN

- Not wanting to use a certain part of the body—for example, favoring a particular paw.
- Not wanting to eat.
- Not wanting (or being unable) to jump during play.
- Not jumping directly onto the couch or windowsill, but taking smaller steps instead.
- Not wanting (or being unable) to sit or lie down in a relaxed position.
- Suddenly becoming aggressive without a visible reason.
- Becoming aggressive when you touch him in a certain spot.
- Licking or grooming a certain part of his body a lot.
- Hissing or growling at a certain part of his body.
- Going outside the litterbox.
- Retreating, or even hiding.
- In extreme cases, panting (rather like a dog).

SIGNS OF A TOOTHACHE

- Smelly breath.
- Drooling.
- Swelling or bleeding of the gums.
- Dropping food while eating.
- Refusing to eat hard kibble.
- Pawing the mouth regularly.
- Showing aggression when touched near the mouth.
- Losing weight (not eating enough).
- Sometimes, even screaming when eating.

HOW CAN I TELL IF MY CAT IS SICK?

Recognizing a sick cat is nearly as difficult as recognizing one who's in pain. The better you know your cat, the sooner you'll notice that something is wrong. I describe some symptoms of illness below, but the most important thing is to follow your gut: If your instincts tell you that "something's up" with your cat, take her to the vet as soon as possible!

SYMPTOMS TO WATCH FOR

- A runny nose, sniffles, or sneezing mean your cat is sick—but contrary to popular belief, a wet or dry nose doesn't say much about your cat's health.

- Showing the "third eyelid" is a clear signal that your cat isn't feeling well. (This is the *nictitating membrane*, a cloudy white layer that closes across the eyeball starting from the inner corner.)

- A dull or unkempt coat, that is, your cat's fur sticks up rather than lying smoothly against her skin. (If your cat has stopped grooming herself, or is grooming more often or more fanatically, that's always a reason for concern.)

- Losing weight.

- Eating or drinking more, or not eating at all.

- Stinky breath or another body odor.

- Changes in urine or poop (diarrhea, constipation, or a different smell or color).

- Vomiting a lot.

- Listlessness, not wanting to play, or hiding.

- Becoming needy or aloof.

- Never lying down at ease—staying upright instead, or crouching.

- A stuffed-up nose, coughing, or difficulty swallowing.

- Holding her head sideways, carrying her tail differently, or no longer raising her tail in the air as a greeting.

- Staggering or standing uncertainly on her paws.

HOW TO RECOGNIZE URINARY PROBLEMS

When your cat pees outside his box, there's often a medical cause. It's an oft-repeated misunderstanding that you can tell whether a cat has a UTI from his appearance or how often he pees. Unfortunately, this isn't true—which leads to many cats' issues going untreated for a long time, leaving them to walk around in unnecessary pain.

SYMPTOMS TO WATCH FOR

These are the best-known and most commonly occurring symptoms of a urinary tract infection or related problem:

- Peeing in the house (outside the litterbox).

- Peeing often, just a little bit each time.

- Going to the litterbox regularly but not being able to pee.

- Not peeing at all. (This is an emergency; get to the vet right away!)

- Meowing or "whining" while urinating.

- Straining while using the litterbox.

- Blood in the urine.

- Peeing on the floor in front of you. (This isn't the ultimate show of disrespect; rather, it's a call for help from your cat.)

HIDDEN PROBLEMS

Even if you don't see any of the symptoms listed above, that doesn't mean your cat can't have a urinary problem or cystitis (bladder inflammation). Consider the following:

- Sometimes a cat won't show any symptoms beyond peeing in the house!

- Blood in the urine can't usually be seen with the naked eye.

- Spraying can also be a sign of bladder trouble.

There are many cats who keep going in the litterbox like a good kitty despite being ill. That's why you should be on the lookout for these symptoms as well:

- Licking her belly until it's bald.

- Grooming under her tail (too) often.

- Pacing back and forth anxiously, or meowing or walking around before using the litterbox (if she never used to do this before).

Sometimes a cat doesn't show any symptoms of bladder trouble besides peeing in the house!

Urinary problems are quite common in cats and unfortunately not always easy to detect, as discussed. The best way to help your kitty is by prevention:

- Provide enough moisture in her diet: Offer wet food, choose the right water bowl (and location), and keep it topped up with fresh water (see page 120).

- Litterbox hesitation can cause a cat to hold his pee (see page 96), which in turn can lead to too-concentrated urine that forms "crystals" and, ultimately, blockage. Paying extra attention to the litterbox not only keeps your kitty happy, it keeps him healthy too!

HOW TO GIVE A CAT MEDICINE

So you've been to the vet and they prescribed a daily pill for your kitty. Do you have a pit in your stomach just thinking about persuading him to take it?

OPEN WIDE!

Giving pills will be much easier if you've already taught your cat to let you look in his mouth, starting when he was a kitten (see page 157). Unfortunately, few cat owners do this—but the following tips can still help.

SNEAKING MEDS INTO A SNACK

The easiest way to give your cat a pill is to grind it up and mix it in with her wet food (after checking with your veterinarian that it's OK to do so). Note that your cat needs to like her food enough that she won't mind if you mix something into it. And be careful with hiding medicine in food: This usually works with worm or flea pills, but some medications have such a bitter taste that your cat won't want to eat her food anymore.

To keep your cat from becoming distrustful of her dinner, it's a good idea to mix her medication into a different type of food than she usually eats. Putting one or two crumbled-up treats on top of her food conceals the smell and taste of her medicine even better.

"PILLING" YOUR CAT

If hiding medicine in his food doesn't work, but your cat is fairly calm, you can often put a pill directly in his mouth. To start, hold your cat in your lap or arms, or put him on a table to position his mouth at a convenient height.

This is easiest with two people: One holds the cat, and the other one presses on his cheeks with the thumb and index finger of one hand so that he opens his mouth. Alternatively, you can work your finger between your cat's front teeth and gently pull his lower jaw open; this is the method veterinarians use.

With your free hand, push the pill inside your cat's mouth (as far back as possible) and watch for him to swallow. Right afterward, give your cat something to drink or carefully drip some water into his mouth; this prevents the pill from getting stuck in his throat or esophagus and causing irritation. Pay close attention to make sure your cat doesn't spit out his pill after a little while! (If he does, try a different strategy with a new pill. . . .)

You can also use a tablet syringe or "pill popper" to administer medicine; there are even syringes you can fill with water that let you give the pill and "chase" it all in one go.

If your cat has been prescribed a long course of medication, always give him a treat after each dose. He won't appreciate the pill, but he'll learn to love the reward!

Giving pills can be a tremendous challenge

SWADDLING

With many cats, the above method doesn't work, or only works for a time. After a while, a cat understands what's coming next and stops letting you pick him up, which can turn "pill time" into a real battle. At this point you may have to wrap him up in a towel or sweater, but this will quickly become uncomfortable for him—and you still have to pick him up in the first place.

STRESS-FREE PILLS

The tricks above won't be enough to convince a nervous or frightened cat to take her meds. Winning this battle comes down to being smarter than your cat and slipping the pill to her without her noticing. Below are additional methods you can try—but talk to your veterinarian first to make sure they're compatible with your cat's medicine.

- Hide the pill in a small ball of pâté (or another soft, gourmet treat). Freeze it, then let the outside thaw a bit before use. Freezing the treat means your cat won't notice the hard pill at the center, and it eliminates a lot of the nasty pill flavor.

- Grind up the pill in a "pill crusher" or between two spoons, then mix it into a sticky food with a strong taste (such as liverwurst, soft cheese, peanut butter, or a bit of canned tuna in water).

- Use a product like Greenies Pill Pockets: These tasty treats can be wrapped around the pill to hide it. Soft chewing sticks are also ideal for concealing pills.

When following any of these methods, give your cat three treats in succession: first one *without* a pill, then the treat that's hiding the pill, and then a pill-less treat to finish.

Use your imagination and switch up your techniques: As soon as your cat smells or tastes something she doesn't trust, you'll have to come up with something different next time!

How to hide that "medicine smell"

When you're molding a soft treat around a pill to hide it, you may accidentally transfer the smell of the pill to the treat. To avoid this, use tweezers (rather than your fingertips) to pick up the pill. That is, use your hands to open the pill pocket or cut into the chewing stick, then place the pill inside using tweezers, and finally press the treat closed with your fingers.

DON'T STAGE A CAT-NAPPING . . .

It's a really bad idea to snatch your cat for "pill time" by pouncing on her when she's lying in her favorite place or using the litterbox. This can turn her safe place into a source of stress, or teach her to avoid her box.

. . . AND DON'T DESPAIR!

Whatever happens, remain calm! If medicating your cat really stresses her out, the cure may be worse than the disease. If you can't find a workable method, talk to your veterinarian. Some medications can be put into a liquid "suspension" and mixed into your cat's wet food.

THE HAPPY CAT CHECKLIST

If your cat were in charge, he would give you this wishlist!

FOOD (page 108)

☐ Multiple (preferably four) small portions per day.

☐ Serving sizes suited to your cat's age and weight.

☐ A quiet place to eat that isn't next to the litterbox or water bowl.

☐ In multi-cat households, food bowls that aren't too close together.

☐ A puzzle feeder instead of a food bowl, if your cat enjoys it.

WATER (page 120)

☐ A water bowl that's ceramic or stainless steel, not plastic.

☐ A water bowl that's low and broad so your cat doesn't bump his whiskers.

☐ The water bowl is at least six feet away from the food bowl.

☐ Multiple water bowls distributed throughout the house.

☐ Fresh water every day.

THE LITTERBOX (page 96)

☐ A clean litterbox: Scoop out the pee and poop at least once a day.

☐ Preferably multiple litterboxes, even if you have only one cat.

☐ A litterbox that's big enough.

☐ A litterbox without a flap.

☐ Kitty litter with a fine, soft texture and without added scents.

☐ The litterbox is in a quiet, easily accessible location.

☐ No air fresheners, sprays, or incense in or near the litterbox.

SLEEP (page 104)

☐ A calm place to sleep in, where your cat won't be woken up to cuddle.

☐ Multiple good sleeping places to choose from.

☐ His own sleeping place that he doesn't have to share with other cats.

SCRATCHING (page 88)

☐ A scratching post or board that's tall enough for your cat to stretch out fully.

☐ A stable scratching post.

☐ Multiple scratching options in the house, especially in multi-cat households.

☐ Scratching posts along or near your cat's usual walking path.

☐ Horizontal or vertical scratching options, depending on your cat's preference.

PLAYING (page 178)

☐ A set playtime every day, lasting at least a few minutes, even for adult cats.

☐ Play that challenges your cat and lets him have fun running or jumping.

☐ Toys aren't left lying around the house, but are switched out every other day.

☐ New stimuli (like a new cardboard box) appear on a regular basis.

DE-STRESSING (page 34)

☐ Teach your cat not to be afraid of the cat carrier or vacuum cleaner.

☐ Teach your cat to let you brush his coat and look in his mouth without fear.

☐ Don't pick up your cat if he doesn't want you to.

☐ Be aware of your cat's body language, and respect his boundaries when petting him.

☐ Don't punish your cat; instead, teach him new behaviors.

☐ Take a good look at whether relationships between your cats are causing them stress. Provide sufficient space and separate resources for each cat.

☐ Don't add new cats to a harmonious group.

HEALTH (page 200)

☐ Take your cat to the vet every year for a checkup.

☐ Be on the lookout for behavioral changes that could indicate pain.

☐ Don't let your cat become overweight!

. . . and that's how to "check every box" for your cat!

SOURCES

Beaver, B. V. *Feline Behavior: A Guide for Veterinarians,* 2nd ed. St. Louis, MO: Saunders, 2003.

Bol, S., J. Caspers, L. Buckingham, G. D. Anderson-Shelton, C. Ridgway, C. A. Buffington, S. Schulz, and E. M. Bunnik. "Responsiveness of cats (*Felidae*) to silver vine (*Actinidia polygama*), Tatarian honeysuckle (*Lonicera tatarica*), valerian (*Valeriana officinalis*) and catnip (*Nepeta cataria*)." *BMC Veterinary Research* 13.1 (2017): 70.

Bradshaw, J. W. S., *Cat Sense: How the New Feline Science Can Make You a Better Friend to Your Pet.* New York: Basic Books, 2013.

———— and S. Ellis. *The Trainable Cat: A Practical Guide to Making Life Happier for You and Your Cat.* New York: Basic Books, 2016.

————, R. A. Casey, and S. L. Brown. *The Behaviour of the Domestic Cat,* 2nd ed. Wallingford, Oxfordshire: CABI, 2012.

————, and R. E. Lovett. "Dominance hierarchies in domestic cats: useful construct or bad habit?" *Proceedings of the British Society of Animal Science* (2003): 16.

Chesler, P. "Maternal influence in learning by observation in kittens." *Science* 166.3907 (1969): 901–903.

Deng, P., E. Iwazaki, S. A. Suchy, M. R. Pallotto, and K. S. Swanson. "Effects of feeding frequency and dietary water content on voluntary physical activity in healthy adult cats." *Journal of Animal Science* 92.3 (2014): 1271–1277.

Ellis, S. L. H., V. Swindell, and O. H. P. Burman. "Human classification of context-related vocalizations emitted by familiar and unfamiliar domestic cats: an exploratory study." *Anthrozoös* 28.4 (2015): 625–634.

Godoy, M. R. C. de, K. Ochi, L. F. de Oliveira Mateus, A. C. C. de Justino, and K. S. Swanson. "Feeding frequency, but not dietary water content, affects voluntary physical activity in young lean adult female cats." *Journal of Animal Science* 93.5 (2015): 2597–2601.

Horowitz, A. "Disambiguating the 'guilty look': salient prompts to a familiar dog behaviour." *Behavioural Processes* 81.3 (2009): 447–452.

Macdonald, D. W., and P. J. Apps. "The social behaviour of a group of semi-dependent farm cats, *Felis catus*: a progress report." *Carnivore Genetics Newsletter* 3.7 (1978): 256–268.

————, N. Yamaguchi, and G. Kerby. "Group-living in the domestic cat: its sociobiology and epidemiology." In *The Domestic Cat: The Biology of Its Behaviour,* 2nd ed., edited by D. C. Turner and P. Bateson, 95–118. Cambridge: Cambridge University Press, 2000.

Martell-Moran, N. K., M. Solano, and H. G. Townsend. "Pain and adverse behavior in declawed cats." *Journal of Feline Medicine and Surgery* 20.4 (2018): 280–288.

McComb, K., A. M. Taylor, C. Wilson, and B. D. Charlton. "The cry embedded within the purr." *Current Biology* 19.13 (2009): 507–508.

McCune, S. "The impact of paternity and early socialisation on the development of cats' behaviour to people and novel objects." *Applied Animal Behaviour Science* 45.1–2 (1995): 109–124.

McGowan, R. T. S., J. J. Ellis, M. K. Bensky, and F. Martin. "The ins and outs of the litter box: A detailed ethogram of cat elimination behavior in two contrasting environments." *Applied Animal Behaviour Science* 194 (2017): 67–78.

Ostojíc, L., M. Tkalčić, and N. S. Clayton. "Are owners' reports of their dogs' 'guilty look' influenced by the dogs' action and evidence of the misdeed?" *Behavioural Processes* 111 (2015): 97–100.

Overall, K. L. *Manual of Clinical Behavioral Medicine for Dogs and Cats.* St. Louis, MO: Elsevier, 2013.

Panksepp, J. "Can PLAY diminish ADHD and facilitate the construction of the social brain?" *Journal of the Canadian Academy of Child and Adolescent Psychiatry* 16.2 (2007): 57–66.

Pisa, P. E., and C. Agrillo. "Quantity discrimination in felines: a preliminary investigation of the domestic cat (*Felis silvestris catus*)." *Journal of Ethology* 27.2 (2009): 289–293.

Raihani, G., A. Rodríguez, A. Saldaña, M. Guarneros, and R. Hudson. "A proposal for assessing individual differences in behaviour during early development in the domestic cat." *Applied Animal Behaviour Science* 154 (2014): 48–56.

Rochlitz, I. *The Welfare of Cats.* Dordrecht: Springer, 2007.

Schultz, J. L., P. A. Antender, and S. Zawistowski. *Companion Animal Response to the Loss of an Animal Companion.* New York: The American Society for the Prevention of Cruelty to Animals, 1996.

Shreve, K. R. V., and M. A. R. Udell. "Stress, security, and scent: the influence of chemical signals on the social lives of domestic cats and implications for applied settings." *Applied Animal Behaviour Science* 187 (2017): 69–76.

Pryor, K., *Clicker Training for Cats.* Waltham, MA: Karen Pryor Clicker Training/ Sunshine Books, Inc., 2003.

Turner, D. C., and P. Bateson. *The Domestic Cat: The Biology of Its Behaviour,* 3rd ed. Cambridge: Cambridge University Press, 2014.

———, J. Feaver, M. Mendl, and P. Bateson. "Variation in domestic cat behaviour towards humans: A paternal effect." *Animal Behaviour* 34.6 (1986): 1890–1892.

Wells, D. L., and S. Millsopp. "Lateralized behaviour in the domestic cat, *Felis silvestris catus.*" *Animal Behaviour* 78.2 (2009): 537–541.

INDEX

THANK YOU

I would like to thank my colleagues José Dieker and Jasmien Jansen for their valuable additions and critical eyes, and my colleague Maggie Ruitenberg for her contributions on purebred cats. Irene van Belzen made an entire day available so Erwin Puts could photograph the amazing Bengals from her cattery. I am also thankful to Sure PetCare for their contribution.

Editor Madeleine Gimpel brought structure to the final Dutch version. A big thank you, also, to my American editors Karen Giangreco and Hannah Matuszak for their great questions!

And, of course, I am very thankful to my partner, who continues to support me, and our dear cat Dennis, who missed out on some cuddling while I was writing this.

This book would not exist without the many sweet, fun, special, and inspiring cats I have met or treated in the past years, and from whom I have learned so much!

This book is dedicated to Erwin and Dennis, who died within days of each other during the making of the American edition. You will be missed very much.

ABOUT THE AUTHOR

LIESBETH PUTS is an internationally certified animal behaviorist specializing in cats. She also holds a degree in social psychology from Utrecht University. She has been a cat parent since 1976, a behavioral therapist since 2008, and a cat blogger (read by thousands of fans in her native Netherlands) since 2012. She lives in Utrecht.